MW00625583

What Are People Saying About *Deconstructing Hell?*

"I first learned about hell in Catholic school when I was in third grade. The nun was surprisingly graphic. For the next several years, I was terrified of God and had reoccurring nightmares of being sent to hell. I could not understand how we could say "God is love" if God is capable of inflicting never-ending pain on people! I now consider the teaching that hell involves eternal conscious suffering (ECS) to be a monstrous assault on God's good character and an affliction on the psyche to all who come to believe it, which is why I am excited to recommend *Deconstructing Hell*. Each of the remarkable essays in this impressively diverse collection deconstructs ECS from a different perspective in a compelling way. The sooner this nightmarish teaching is laid to rest, the better!"

—Gregory Boyd, *God of the Possible,*
Is God to Blame, Cross Vision

"*Deconstructing Hell* insightfully shows that the common idea of hell as eternal conscious torment is unbiblical, makes God immoral, and causes trauma in people. This work examines the biblical material, the theology behind hell, the range of alternative views, and, importantly, the serious damage belief in hell has had on people. It shines a bright light on this hideous teaching and will help people move away from a dark, fear-based religion towards the true God who deeply cares for everyone."

—John Sanders, *The Openness of God,*
The God Who Risks

"In *Deconstructing Hell*, each author has made a valuable contribution to the discussion of a "hot topic" that has divided many. Thankfully, these voices bring more light than heat to the matter. Maybe because it's hard to argue with orthodoxy and Scripture."

—Steve McVey, *The Secret of Grace, Gracewalk*

Deconstructing Hell is a "hell of a book!" Like a prism, it presents and challenges images of eternal torment from a variety of perspectives—theological, historical, psychological, spiritual, and autobiographical—and from a variety of voices—scholarly, lay, ministerial, female and male. It asks hard questions and does not give ready-made answers. This is a book for questioners and seekers, for persons from whom the doctrine of eternal torment is an insult to the vision of a loving God and a source of terror and alienation. This book challenges the belief that God needs hell to be just, and that God's love is compatible with torture. Beyond doctrines of the divine abuser so dear to certain strains of conservative Christianity is the open and relational God to whom all hearts are open, and all desires known, the one whose love companions us in life and death and beyond, and whose love never ends for each and all of us.

—Bruce Epperly, *The Elephant is Running,*
Messy Incarnation

Deconstructing
Hell

Open and Relational Responses to the
Doctrine of Eternal Conscious Torment

Chad Bahl, editor

Copyright © 2023 by Chad Bahl and SacraSage Press

All rights reserved. This book or any portion thereof may not be reproduced or used in any manner whatsoever without the express written permission of the publisher except for the use of brief quotations in a book review or scholarly journal.

Print ISBN 978-1-948609-77-7
Ebook ISBN 978-1-948609-78-4

Printed in the United States of America
Library of Congress Cataloguing-in-Publication Data

Deconstructing Hell: Open and Relational Responses to the Doctrine of Eternal Conscious Torment / Chad Bahl

To Christy and Leah.
May you always be led by love.

Table of Contents

How should I begin? Should I treat the subject in the calm way one would when dealing with another issue? Would it be right to pretend to be calm when I am not? To begin calmly would not really communicate a full account of my response. I do not feel calm about the traditional doctrine of hell, and so I will not pretend. Indeed, how can anyone with the milk of human kindness in him remain calm contemplating such an idea as this? Now I realize that in admitting this I am playing into the hands of the critics, when I admit how disturbed the doctrine makes me. They will be able to say that I have adopted arguments on the basis of sentimentality and a subjective sense of moral outrage. Nonetheless, I will take the risk of beginning at the point of my outrage and hope people will hear me and not put it down to sentimentality.

Let me say at the outset that I consider the concept of hell as endless torment in body and mind an outrageous doctrine, a theological and moral enormity. How can Christians possibly project a deity of such cruelty and vindictiveness whose ways include inflicting everlasting torture upon his creatures however sinful they may have been? Surely a God who would do such a thing is more nearly like Satan than like God, at least by any ordinary moral standards, and by the gospel itself. How can we possibly preach that God has so arranged things that a number of his creatures will undergo physical and mental agony through unending time? Is this not a most disturbing concept that needs some second thoughts? Surely the God and Father of our Lord Jesus Christ is no fiend; torturing people without end is not what our God does. Does the one who told us to love our enemies intend to wreak vengeance on his own enemies for all eternity? As H. Kung appropriately asks, "What would we think of a human being who satisfied his thirst for revenge so implacably and insatiably?"

Having said that, I am ready to discuss the question rationally…

—Clark Pinnock, *The Destruction of the Finally Impenitent*

PREFACE

A Doctrine Under Fire

Doctrine Under Fire

The preceding quote was borrowed from the late theologian, Clark Pinnock, in the introduction to his famous refutation of the doctrine of eternal conscious torment. Though this book intends to be a logical and even-handed response to the eternal suffering motif, Pinnock captures for all of us the sense of moral indignation that should be kindled in everyone who objectively contemplates the implications of holding what has sadly become the Church's majority view.

Emphasis on "become." For as early as the Apostolic Fathers of the second century A.D. (Clement of Rome, Ignatius of Antioch, Polycarp, etc.) to Clement of Alexandria and Origen of the third century, we see clear evidence of the emergence of three views of final punishment (the second and third being those of conditional immortality and universalism).[1] The doctrine of eternal suffering may have dominated Christian thought for the past sixteen centuries, but the preaching of everlasting hellfire only picked up steam (if you will) the further out we got from those closest to the canonical authors.

---

1. Edward Fudge, "The Fire That Consumes" (*Fallbrook, CA: Verdict Publications*, 1982), 313-41.

From Augustine of Hippo to John Calvin to Wayne Grudem, when the afterlife is spoken of, the torments of the sinful have been referenced as though the matter was settled. We find one of history's most well-known orators of fire and brimstone in 18th century's Jonathan Edwards. His sermon, *Sinners in the Hands of an Angry God*, illustrates the traditionalist sentiment well:

> The God that holds you over the pit of hell, much as one holds a spider or some loathsome insect over the fire, abhors you, and is dreadfully provoked; his wrath towards you burns like fire; he looks upon you as worthy of nothing else, but to be cast into the fire…you are ten thousand times so abominable in his eyes, as the most hateful and venomous serpent is in ours…there is laid in the very nature of carnal men a foundation for the torments of hell.[2]

Reflection on the above quote evokes feelings of both sadness and anger, as it fails spectacularly to reflect the loving heart of God and the inherent value placed upon His creation, seen throughout the Scripture. This sort of fear mongering may have been a compelling tactic centuries ago, but it certainly is not today. In a post-modern era in which skepticism and intellectualism reign supreme, very few people are frightened by the tired vision of a devil, a pitchfork and a burning pit. Most, to the contrary, are rather turned off by it. This may be seen from the lack of affinity passers-by have towards the occasional angry preacher on a street corner to the growing number of apologists for atheism who use such teachings as leverage to advocate against Christianity. If the threat of eternal torment was a successful means of delivering the Good News to those in need, one would think more people would be receptive to the message.

---

2. Jonathan Edwards, "Sinners in the Hands of an Angry God. A Sermon Preached at Enfield, July 8th, 1741," (1741).

But this is not the case. Most thoughtful people in our culture today are quite repulsed by the concept of what they see as such an unscrupulous God. Pastor and author Gregory Boyd published a series of dialogues that he and his father exchanged regarding the Christian faith in his book *Letters from a Skeptic*. In this publication, Boyd converses with his atheist father in hopes of introducing him to faith in God. As the book comes to an end, the last major issue Boyd's father could not overcome was the contradiction he found between a loving God and the punishment of eternal suffering. A glimpse of this particular letter will be illustrative:

> Your last letter put my mind at ease about who is going to hell, but it didn't address the problem of hell itself. This is really the more fundamental question...Now tell me, what the hell (excuse the pun) would be the purpose of torturing someone eternally? What's the point? Obviously, there's no lesson to be learned. So it just does not make sense to me Greg. And I'm just not at the point where I can "suspend" judgement on this. The character of God is on trial in my life, and this is very relevant evidence that needs to be considered.[3]

I am hoping I'm not spoiling the end of a good read to say that after Greg presents his dad with what will be argued in Chapter six of this book as a biblical alternative to the traditionalist view, Mr. Boyd ceases to find the doctrine of hell a barrier to faith and decides to yield his life to following the loving God of the Bible.

Christian Deconstruction

Although this book is limited in scope to essays addressing the eternal conscious torment view of hell, it has evolved in concept out of

---

3. Gregory A. Boyd and Edward Boyd, *Letters from a Skeptic: A Son Wrestles with His Father's Questions about Christianity* (Colorado Springs, CO: David C Cook, 2010), 160.

the larger process of Christian deconstruction happening within the Church today. Christianity entails the fundamental belief that man is limited in knowledge compared to God's unlimited understanding. Scripture often draws on this contrast in an explicit manner:

- Isaiah 55: 8-9—"For my thoughts are not your thoughts, neither are my ways your ways," declares the Lord. "As the heavens are higher than the earth, so my ways are higher than your ways and my thoughts higher than your thoughts."

- Job 38: 1-4—Then the Lord spoke to Job out of the storm. He said, "Who is this that obscures my plans with words without knowledge? Prepare to defend yourself; I will question you and you shall answer me. Where were you when I laid the earth's foundation? Tell me if you understand."

- And of course, Romans 11:33-36—Oh, the depth of the riches of the wisdom and knowledge of God! How unsearchable his judgements and his paths beyond tracing out! Who has known the mind of the Lord? Or who has been his counselor? Who has ever given to God that God should repay them? For from him and to him and through him are all things. To him be the glory forever! Amen.

And with limited knowledge comes the acknowledgement that, on occasion, even with the most elaborate and well-grounded systematic theology, we will get things wrong about God—that the Church will get things wrong about God. David Basinger, in his book *The Case for Free Will Theism*, speaks out against what he calls "Bunker Theology."[4] Too often, once we have formulated a view of the divine, we only approach our reading of the Bible in such a way that seeks to support those views, however incorrect they may be. If a passage seems to contradict our way of thinking, we assume there must be an alternative explanation: "Perhaps that's not really what

---

4. David Bassinger, *The Case for Free Will Theism: A Philosophical Assessment* (Downers Grove, IL: InterVarsity, 2010), 11-20.

the original text actually says." Or we just chalk up the apparent contradiction to the inexplicable "mysteries of God." I would hope, for myself, never to feel so confident in my theology as not to be willing to correct a wrong view once presented with compelling evidence.

I will admit at the outset that this sort of reframing isn't always the easiest approach to theological study. Being willing to alter what we believe about God can sometimes feel like acknowledging that we never truly knew God in the first place. As Clark Pinnock appropriately put it, "...The reconsidering of one's model of God [can] be a delicate issue... It may feel as if, when a familiar way of thinking about God is questioned, God himself is lost or has become distant." But this doesn't have to stay the case. As he goes on to state, "The experience of re-conceptualizing can be positive. After the initial anxiety of rethinking, one will find God again in a fresh way around the next bend in the reflective road."[5]

As uncomfortable as reconceptualizing our theology can be, at times it is eminently necessary. Occasionally, we will not be able to square our reading of the Bible with sound reasoning, both of which have been granted to us by our Creator. At times, we will discover contradictory themes in Scripture that we feel compelled to reconcile. And sometimes, we will uncover distortions of truth that may shake the very foundations of our belief systems. In which case, we must deconstruct for fear of losing faith altogether. The authors of this book make the claim that the eternal conscious torment view of hell, for many, is this latter option.

We must encourage, not judge, such deconstructing. For the journey to truth is among the most fundamental of Christian endeavors. I am not claiming that everything is subject to mere opinion (1 Corinthians 3:10-14; 15:3-8), but we are to seek truth (Matthew 7:7-8), fact check (Acts 17:11), approach revelation with skepticism (1 John 4:1), in cooperation with others (Proverbs 17:7),

---

5. Clark H. Pinnock, "Systematic Theology" in *The Openness of God: A Biblical Challenge to the Traditional Understanding of God*, Clark H. Pinnock, et al. (Downers Grove, IL: Intervarsity, 2010), 104.

valuing differing perspectives (Proverbs 15:22) and appreciating all
the God has revealed to those around us (John 14:26). This is the
high calling and precious joy of the Bride seeking the Bridegroom.

Deconstructing Hell

What follows is a collection of essays by writers who wish to share
their journeys in deconstructing hell. As you travel with us, you
may notice that this book gets quite messy, as deconstruction often
can be. No author within shares the exact same theology as another.
We come from backgrounds ranging from Process to Mainline
Christian to Evangelical. We advocate for various alternatives to
the traditional view spanning from Conditional Immortality to
Universal Restoration to alternative options (such as Thomas Jay
Oord's Relentless Love Theory), to those that are less well-defined.[6]
We approach our arguments from the perspective of storytellers,
philosophers, historians and theologians. What is important is that
we are united in agreement that the doctrine of eternal suffering is
perhaps the most detestable, sustained claim of antiquity and that
it fails decisively at conveying the loving heart of the God of the
Bible.

Renowned atheist Richard Dawkins and I don't agree on much,
but his quote resonates: "I can't think of many people who deserve
to go to hell, but people who teach its existence to vulnerable children are prime candidates."[7]

Open and Relational

The reader will notice that *Deconstructing Hell* has been billed as an
"open and relational response" to the doctrine of eternal conscious

---

6. For more on this, see Chapter 14 of this present volume, *God's Glory as Relentless Love*,
by Thomas Jay Oord.

7. Richard Dawkins (@RichardDawkins), Twitter, May 26, 2013, https://twitter.com/
richarddawkins/status/338593323885395968.

torment. Simply put, open and relational theology entails two premises:

1. God experiences time moment by moment (is open)

2. God, us, and creation relate, so that everyone gives and receives (is relational)

Most open and relational thinkers also affirm additional ideas, including love as an ultimate ethic, the importance of the synthesis of science and faith, libertarian creaturely freedom and more.

For our purposes, the context of open and relational theology sets the stage well to contrast the implications of the doctrine of eternal conscious torment with the biblical presentation of a God of love. With that said, it should be noted that most, but not all authors included in the present volume would include themselves fully within the open and relational camp.

A Welcoming Invitation

The authors of this book extend an invitation to all. To those who find themselves deconstructing their faith, you are welcome. To those who cannot countenance a God who would subject His creation to eternal suffering, you are welcome. To those who are simply unsure what they believe regarding the biblical view of hell, you are welcome.

May the God of love and grace bless your journey.

—Chad

CHAPTER 1

To Hell and Back: A History of Hell

Robert D. Cornwall

Even today a large percentage of Christians believe that upon our deaths, we will face judgment leading either to eternal life in heaven/paradise or eternal punishment/suffering in hell. While growing numbers of Christians are rejecting this view, it remains prevalent. So, how did we get here? What is the way forward, especially in the context of an "open and relational theology"? For my part, my focus will be on the prior question, but as we all have our own views of such things, I will mention my own perspective as an addendum to the end of the article. To provide an answer to how we got here, we need to go back to the roots of the Christian movement and trace the development of these ideas forward. Those roots include ancient Judaism (both in the Old Testament and extra-canonical texts) and Greco-Roman understandings of the afterlife. These questions form part of the theological category of eschatology.[1]

It is helpful if we start with a definition of hell so that we are on the same page. Alan Bernstein defines hell as "a divinely sanctioned place of eternal torment for the wicked. It is 'divinely sanctioned'

---

1. For more see Robert D. Cornwall and Ronald J. Allen, *Second Thoughts About the Second Coming: A Guide to the Many Ways Christians Interpret the Second Coming of Jesus* (Louisville, KY: Westminster John Knox Press, 2023).

because the God (or, the gods) who established it could have refrained from creating it and could at any time demolish it. Its existence depends on some divinely established purpose."[2] The question
that will arise as time passes concerns the nature of that divinely
established purpose.

The Afterlife and Ancient Judaism

I am using the term "ancient Judaism" in a way that includes the
Old Testament while also including extra-biblical materials. The
idea of hell is not present in the earliest Old Testament documents.
The concept of *Sheol,* as found in the Old Testament, can refer to
a grave or a place of post-death existence. Much like the Greek
concept of Hades, it is the abode of all the dead and not necessarily a place of judgment. At least in their origins, neither *Sheol* nor
Hades are the equivalent of hell. *Sheol,* like Hades, is either a banal
nether world where one exists as a disembodied shade or the grave.
With early Judaism, immortality is not innate as in an immortal
soul. Immortality is essentially a gift of God. Therefore, unless God
chooses to raise a person from the dead when they die, they cease
to exist. Additionally, Daniel is the first and only Old Testament
book to speak of the resurrection of the dead, and Daniel is an
apocalyptic text that envisions the resurrection taking place at the
end of time.

While the idea of hell is largely absent from the Old Testament,
there are hints of an afterlife. Consider the witch of Endor's sum-
moning of Samuel for Saul (1 Sam. 28:8-19), but there is still no
concept of eternal punishment. However, Ezekiel envisions a form
of segregation of the righteous and wicked in *Sheol,* with God casting Egypt and other oppressive powers into the pit that lies in the
world below (Ezek. 32:18-21). Isaiah consigns Babylon to a similar fate (Isa. 14:15-20). While the Greek term *Gehenna* (Hebrew:

---

2. Alan E. Bernstein, *The Formation of Hell: Death and Retribution in the Ancient and
Early Christian Worlds* (Ithaca, NY: Cornell University Press, 1993), 3.

Ge-Hinnom, Valley of Hinnom) is eventually identified as hell, it's not the equivalent of Hades (*Sheol*). Gehenna was originally connected to the sacrificial offerings to the god Molech. While King Ahaz embraced these offerings, (2 Kings 16:3), Josiah later banned them (2 Kings 23:10). Nevertheless, the valley came to be associated with burning, shame, and wickedness (Jer. 7, 19).

The idea of resurrection first emerges in the Old Testament with Daniel (165 B.C.E.). This is also the period in which the idea of an immortal soul begins to enter the conversation in ancient Judaism. While Daniel offers us an apocalyptic vision of God's judgment and the possibility of resurrection, the idea reaches its fuller development in deuterocanonical and apocryphal texts such as 1 Enoch. Especially in the section known as the "Book of Watchers," we begin to see descriptions of the afterlife, divine judgment, and forms of punishment. In 1 Enoch, the angel Raphael takes Enoch to see the place where the souls of the dead reside until the day of judgment. For some, there will be delightful places for human souls to reside (1 Enoch 22:3-5).[3] However, Raphael also reveals to Enoch the fate of the wicked. This is a valley burning with fire where fetters of iron are being prepared for the monarchs and the mighty. According to Raphael, the followers of the angel Azazel will be cast into an abyss. On the day of judgment, the angels Michael, Gabriel, and Raphael, will cast the mighty ones into "a furnace of blazing fire, that the Lord of Spirits may take vengeance on them for their unrighteousness that the Lord of Spirits may be avenged of them for their crimes; because they became ministers of Satan, and seduced those who dwell upon earth" (1 Enoch 53:5-6). It's important to note that the vision suggests the destruction of the wicked, not eternal punishment. We see this as well in the *Psalms of Solomon* "For the life of the righteous is forever but sinners shall be taken away into destruction and their memorial shall never be found" (Ps. Of Sol. 13:11 *New English Translation of the Septuagint*).

---

3. "Book of Enoch," Pseudepigraphia, accessed December 3, 2022, http://www.pseudepigrapha.com/pseudepigrapha/1enoch_all.html#CH22

The two books of Maccabees, especially 2 Maccabees, which date to around 124 B.C.E., are not apocalypses, but they do develop apocalyptic ideas including the future day of judgment, at which time the righteous will be rewarded. However, there is no explicit word concerning eternal punishment for the wicked, only annihilation. 4 Maccabees, which emerged two centuries later, envisions the possibility of death leading to eternal punishment of the wicked, who will be punished after death, even as the faithful were tortured in life.[4]

By the first century C.E., Judaism had produced a more fully developed vision of post-mortem existence. According to Josephus, while the Sadducees, a more conservative aristocratic movement, denied the idea of post-mortem existence, the same was not true for the Pharisees. The Pharisees (Paul, a Pharisee, and Jesus, shared many of the movement's beliefs) believed that the soul survived death and that the soul of a person would receive either an eternal reward or experience eternal punishment in the underworld.[5]

Alan Bernstein offers a helpful summation of why belief in future punishment emerged. He suggests that "belief in punishment after death becomes necessary when no sign of restoration is visible in life." Thus, it is "a manifestation of the sublimated desire for vengeance," and that through "the resurrection all wrong will be punished and not just the wrongs committed by evil doers alive at the time of punishment."[6] Thus, we need to keep in mind the promise of Deuteronomy 32:35-36, that vengeance belongs to God. If this is true, then if vindication doesn't come in this life, surely it must come in the next life.

---

4. Bart Ehrman, *Heaven and Hell: A History of the Afterlife* (New York, NY: Simon and Schuster, 2020), 130-32.

5. Bernstein, *Formation of Hell*, 179.

6. Ibid., 202.

The New Testament and Eternal Punishment

Late Jewish apocalyptic theology provides the foundation for New Testament understandings of life after death, including post-mortem punishment. Texts such as Daniel and 1 Enoch proved influential. While there are suggestions in the New Testament of the possibility of forms of eternal punishment, there are also suggestions that annihilation is the fate of those who oppose Jesus. That appears to be the view of Paul who says little if anything about hell. While early Christianity emerges out of ancient Judaism, it is also influenced by Greek concepts. However, the early Christians, as evidenced by the New Testament, broke with the Greek idea of reality's cyclical nature by envisioning a linear teleological reality. Thus, there is no room here for concepts such as reincarnation, a concept that Plato, for instance, embraced. There is little evidence as well of there being second chances of post-mortem conversion.

For Paul, there is evidence that he was attracted to the idea of universal restoration but ultimately chooses annihilation as the fate of the faithless. His one reference to *Hades* serves as a parallel to the Greek *Thanatos* (death) (1 Cor. 15:54-55). The Gospel of John offers a similar vision, with the wrath of God leading to a denial of eternal life (annihilation).

In the Synoptic Gospels, Jesus does speak of judgment leading to persons being cast into Gehenna. There are references in parables to the wicked being cast into a place where there will be "weeping and gnashing of teeth" (Matt. 24:51; Matt. 25:30). We see the gospel foundations for the concept of hell in passages such as Mark 9:43-48 and Matthew 25:31-46. In the latter passage, where Jesus speaks of the separation of the sheep and the goats, the goats (those who do not serve the Son of Man, are sent to the place of eternal fire reserved for the devil and his angels. Then in verse 46, Jesus reveals that this punishment is eternal. This place of punishment is revealed to be Gehenna. For his part, Luke speaks of Hades in the same way as Matthew and Mark speak of Gehenna (Luke 16:19-31). This passage is the famous parable of Lazarus and the rich man. In that parable, both Lazarus and the rich man are found in Hades, but in different parts of the underworld. The rich man experiences torment while Lazarus sits in the lap of luxury in the presence of Abraham. This is the first reference to eternal punishment in the New Testament.[7]

Our final stop is the Book of Revelation. The question of whether the references there to the Lake of Fire as a destination for the wicked is intended to be interpreted as a place of eternal torment or annihilation, such that to be thrown into the fire ends the possibility of eternal life. The devil experiences eternal torment, but not humans. In Revelation 20:14, those whose names are not written in the Book of Life are thrown into the Lake of Fire, but this is the second death. It does not explicitly suggest eternal punishment.

While there is little evidence in the Bible for eternal punishment, there is enough material here that could be developed further in conversation with Hellenistic thought. As Christianity moved into a Hellenistic world, it imbibed those ideas, including the idea of the immortal soul, and incorporate them into its interpretation of biblical references to judgment.

Eternal Punishment in Early Christianity

One of the earliest descriptions of eternal punishment is found in the second-century apocalyptic work, the "Apocalypse of Peter." It is followed by the "Apocalypse of Paul" (4th-5th centuries). The "Apocalypse of Peter" is the first Christian text to describe a journey through both heaven and hell. The vision developed there proved influential in Dante's vision of hell. While we do not have a complete version of this apocalypse, we know from early Christian writers that it was highly influential. What it depicts is hell as a place of punishment. It describes in detail the punishment of persons in ways reflective of their wickedness. Thus, women judged as adulterers were hung by their hair above a boiling mire, while

---

7. Ehrman, *Heaven and Hell*, 197-202.

men were hung by their feet, with their heads hidden in the mire. Murderers were cast into a place filled with evil creeping things, such as worms, that preyed upon them. The rich who ignored the widows and orphans were sent to a place that was marked by "gravel-stones sharper than swords or any spit, heated with fire, and men and women clad in filthy rages rolled upon them in torment." In other words, they reaped what they sowed.[8]

As with the emergence of visions of postmortem punishment, whether eternal or not, in ancient Judaism, the presence of such ideas in early Christianity was often related to the presence of persecution. Thus, Cyprian of Carthage (third century C.E.), addressing a period of severe persecution, wrote in detail about eternal punishment in hell (Gehenna) being meted out against the persecutors. He encouraged the people to embrace martyrdom with the promise of reward for the faithful and punishment for the persecutor: "Oh, what and how great will that day be at its coming, beloved brethren, when the Lord shall begin to count up His people,…to send the guilty to Gehenna, and to set on fire our persecutors with the perpetual burning of a penal fire, but to pay to us the reward of our faith and devotion!" (Epistle 55:10).[9] In an "Address to Demetrius," he declares that "an ever-burning Gehenna will burn up the condemned, and a punishment devouring with living flames." This torment will continue without end, such that those who persecuted the church will be "compensated by a perpetual spectacle, according to the truth of Holy Scripture, which says, 'Their worm shall not die, and their fire shall not be quenched; and they shall be for a vision to all flesh.'"[10] While Cyprian sought to

---

8. *The Apocryphal New Testament: Being the Apocryphal Gospels, Acts, Epistles, and Apocalypses, with Other Narratives and Fragments,* trans. M.R. James (UK: Clarendon Press, 1926), 509.

9. Cyprian, "To the People of Thibaris, Exhorting to Martyrdom," in *Ante-Nicene Fathers*, eds. Alexander Roberts and James Donaldson, (Grand Rapids, MI: Christian Classics Ethereal Library (CCEL 5) 5:iv.iv.lv. https://ccel.org/ccel/cyprian/epistles/anf05.iv.iv.lv.html.

10. Cyprian, "An Address to Demetrianus," in *Ante-Nicene Fathers Vol. 5*, eds. Alexander Roberts and James Donaldson, (Grand Rapids, MI: Christian Classics Ethereal Library (CCEL 5) iv.v.v. https://ccel.org/ccel/cyprian/epistles/anf05.iv.v.v.html

encourage fellow Christians by promising eternal punishment for
the persecutor, after the legalization of Christianity, texts such as
the "Apocalypse of Paul," which like the much earlier "Apocalypse
of Peter" in its detailed description of hell, focused not on pagan
persecutors and idolators, but slack Christians, unruly church offi-
cers, and heretics. After Constantine, the direst punishments were
meted out to ecclesiastical transgressors.[11]

While some early Christian writers began to develop the idea
of eternal punishment, often in some form of hell, there were other
positions as well. Origen (185-243 C.E.) is well known for envisioning the possibility of some form of universal salvation. He
wrote of the restoration of all things, (Greek: *apokatastasis*). While
Origen's views would be later condemned in the sixth century,
his influence would live on through eastern theologians such as
Gregory of Nyssa (4th century C.E.). For Origen, any postmortem
punishment must be seen as corrective and not permanent, such
that the condition that led to punishment was eliminated.[12] In his
work *Contra Celsum,* Origen distinguished between Sheol/Hades
and Gehenna. The former served as a place where the dead re-
sided until the descent of Jesus as hinted at in 1 Peter 4:6, and
Gehenna, which served as a place of torment. Regarding Hades,
Origen spoke of Jesus, who as a bodiless soul went to Hades to
preach to those in Sheol/Hades who might believe (*Contra Celsum*
2:43).[13] While contemplating the possibility of postmortem punishment, Origen suggested that it might not be permanent. While
evil would be destroyed, everything else would be restored (*Contra
Celsum* 8:72).[14] Gregory of Nyssa, a fourth-century Cappadocian
bishop and theologian, followed Origen in many ways. When
it comes to Hades, he interpreted it in more spiritual terms. He

---

11. Ehrman, *Heaven and Hell,* 261-64.

12. Bernstein, *Formation of Hell,* 308-11.

13. Origen, "Contra Celsum" in *Ante-Nicene Fathers Vol. 5,* eds. Alexander Roberts and
James Donaldson (Buffalo, NY: Christian Literature Publishing Co., 1885) Book 2.
https://www.newadvent.org/fathers/04162.htm.

14. Ibid., Book 8. https://www.newadvent.org/fathers/04168.htm

writes that considering the different parts of the narrative and their meaning, then Hades "is not intended to signify a place with that name. The Scripture must be teaching us that it is some invisible and incorporeal condition of life, in which the soul lives."[15]

If Cyprian envisioned a hellish future for those who persecuted Christians and the Apocalypse of Paul applied that to ecclesiastical offenders, while Origen and Gregory of Nyssa envision Hades and Gehenna either as temporary existences or a spiritual existence (with both being influenced by Platonism), it is Augustine who laid out the vision of eternal punishment that would most influence the later western Church. The primary sources of material from Augustine are found in Book twenty-one of the *City of God* and his *Enchiridion*. While Origen could imagine postmortem correction leading to salvation, Augustine understood purgation as a cleansing of the faithful and not a means to postmortem salvation. Thus, the ultimate destination of the wicked is Gehenna, and that fate is determined before death. One of Augustine's primary concerns is answering the objection that fire consumes and therefore the body and soul upon judgment would be annihilated. Augustine replied to this objection by suggesting that resurrected bodies (all bodies are resurrected before judgment), and therefore these bodies will be affected in the same way as the disembodied souls before the resurrection. Therefore, the fire of hell will cause suffering but not death. As for the objection that eternity is too long, he answered that eternal punishment is an exile that cuts humans off from the City of God. Therefore, since the soul is eternal so are exile and punishment.[16] Now, Augustine did not focus on the gore of eternal punishment as did the "Apocalypse of Peter" and that of Paul, choosing to offer a more intellectually focused argument. In his presentation of his view, he also noted that while the punishment is eternal, its nature will vary by degree depending on the enormity

---

15. Gregory of Nyssa, *On the Soul and the Resurrection (Popular Patristics Series)*, trans. Catharine P. Ross (Crestwood, NY: St Vladimir's Seminary Press, 1993), 69-73.

16. Bernstein, *Formation of Hell*, 318-19.

of the crime. Thus, while all who dwell in Gehenna will burn, the "misery will be more tolerable for some than for others" (*The Enchiridion on Faith, Hope, and Love,* 111).

Medieval Visions of Hell

Augustine serves as a turning point between early Christianity and the medieval church. Origen's vision of the restoration of all things was condemned under Justinian at the Fifth Ecumenical Council held at Constantinople in 553 C.E., which led to the destruction of his Greek texts. At that Council, it was decreed that "if anyone says or holds that the punishment of devils and wicked men is temporary and will eventually cease, that is to say, that devils or the ungodly will be completely restored to their original state: let him be anathema."[17] While Origen's ideas, as they were reinterpreted by persons such as Gregory of Nyssa would persist in the East, in the West Augustine's vision provided the foundation for common beliefs about hell and eternal punishment. While we often think of Dante's vision of hell as defining medieval understandings, Dante was a poet and not a theologian. Thus, we need to attend to the leading medieval theologians, especially Thomas Aquinas.

Most medieval Christians, following Augustine, assumed human beings are infected with original sin, which by itself, warrants condemnation to hell. Grace serves as the foundation for salvation, but three things are necessary if grace is to be sustained: faith, sacraments, and good works. Baptism is the foundation piece because it washes away original sin. From there penance is a necessary step in taking care of the effects of one's own mortal and venial sins. Purgatory emerged in the medieval era as a way for forgivable sins to be answered for after death when satisfaction (the final step of penance) had not been completed in one's lifetime.

---

17. *The Church Teaches: Documents of the Fathers of St. Mary's College* (Rockford, IL: Tan Books, 1973), 345.

Hugh of St. Victor (1096-1141 C. E.) spoke of hell as the place where those "who are confirmed in evil and who have irrecoverably forsaken discipline, and accordingly evil only and the supreme evil is placed there." Hugh understood purgatory to be the middle place between hell and heaven, from which one could ascend "through the merit of righteousness or descend through the guilt of sin."[18] When it comes to the geography of hell (Latin *infernus*), Thomas Aquinas spoke in terms of a four-level subterranean dungeon. Hell proper lay at the bottom of the four levels. It was a place where the perpetually damned suffered torment. Those who dwelled at this level experienced both pain and the loss of sight of God. Above that level stood the level where unbaptized children were housed ("limbo of infants"). They suffered only from the loss of sight of God. Above this level was a place of temporary torment/suffering, also known as purgatory. While those housed at this level lost sight of God and experienced suffering, they did not lose grace and thus could be rescued on the day of judgment if not before. This served as a place where the saints in need of purification received that refining fire. Finally, the level standing above that was the holding place for the saints of the Old Testament ("limbo of the fathers"). This is, according to Thomas, the level of hell visited by Jesus between Good Friday and Easter morning, freeing these saints from limbo.[19]

By the twelfth and thirteenth centuries, purgatory had become an important part of the conversation. As we see with Thomas, there is a form of punishment, but with a corrective element, such that the suffering is not permanent. Thomas believed that one could and should pray for those experiencing purgatory, that they might be released from their sins. One need not pray for the

---

18. Hugh of St. Victor, "On the Sacraments of the Christian Faith," in *A Scholastic Miscellany: Anselm to Ockham (Library of Christian Classics: Ichthus Edition),* ed. Eugene R. Fairweather (Philadelphia, PA: Westminster, 1956), 301-02.

19. Henry Ansgar Kelly, "Hell with Purgatory and Two Limbos: The Geography and Theology of the Underworld," in *Hell and Its Afterlife: Historical and Contemporary Perspectives,* eds. Isabel Moreira and Margaret Toscano (Burlington, VT: Ashgate, 2010), 121, 128.

saints in heaven, as they are already fully cleansed, nor for those in hell, for they are beyond hope. Purgatory offers a third means of experiencing restoration after death. Regarding the geography of purgatory and hell, Thomas assumes they are nearby each other so that both experience the same fire. However, the one in purgatory is further away from the fire and will not endure it forever. So, he writes in response to objections to his view: "The punishment of hell is for the purpose of affliction, wherefore it is called by the names of things that are wont to afflict us here. But the chief purpose of the punishment of Purgatory is to cleanse us from the remains of sin; and consequently, the pain of fire only is ascribed to Purgatory, because fire cleanses and consumes" (*Summa Theologica, Supplement, Appendix II*).[20]

Hell: From the Reformation to the Present

The Reformers carried with them many of the earlier views of the nature and purpose of hell, especially those laid out by Augustine. Thus, they didn't differ much from their Roman Catholic co-religionists. It was understood that hell was a place created by God for the eternal punishment of the wicked. Where early Protestants differed from Catholics was in their rejection of purgatory. Thus, starting with Martin Luther, there were two possible post-death destinations: heaven and hell. While hell played a role in the theology of the Reformers, it wasn't a central concern. For the Reformers, the existence of hell served as a warning of the dangers of sin to one's eternal destiny. Another difference from their medieval predecessors, the Reformers rejected the distinction between deadly and forgivable sin. Every sin could be deadly and every sin is forgivable, through grace. Ultimately, according to Luther, hell can be

---

20. Thomas Aquinas, *Summa theologica*, trans. Fathers of the English Dominican Province (New York: Benziger Brothers, 1920), Illae Suppl. II, Art 2, ad. 2. https://www. newadvent.org/summa/7001.htm

avoided by living by faith in Christ and God's grace.[21] As for John Calvin, his only reference to hell (Gehenna) in the *Institutes of the Christian Religion* noted that "no description can deal adequately with the gravity of God's vengeance against the wicked." Therefore images such as weeping, gnashing of teeth, and unquenchable fire, are used to help people "conceive the lot of the wicked, so we ought especially to fix our thoughts upon this: how wretched it is to be cut off from all fellowship with God" (*Institutes,* 3:25:12).

Before moving into the future, as a Roman Catholic counter-point, consider the Jesuit founder Ignatius of Loyola. The "Fifth Exercise" of his *Spiritual Exercises,* is a "Meditation on Hell." After the usual preparatory prayer, he includes two preludes, five points, and a colloquy. In this exercise, Loyola contemplates the nature of hell and asks, "for an interior sense of the pain suffered by the damned, sot that if through my faults I should forget the love of the Eternal Lord, at least the fear of those pains will serve to keep me from falling into sin." From there he meditates on the nature of the experiences of those consigned to hell, and why they are there. With that, he gives thanks to Christ because Christ has not let him fall into the classes of those consigned to hell. Thus, in many ways similar to the Reformers, he sees the possibility of hell being a warning to remain faithful to Christ.[22]

Pushing further into the future, we come to two figures, one who follows in the path of Calvin, but with more ferocity. That would be Jonathan Edwards, famed for his revival sermon "Sinners in the Hands of an Angry God." The other is John Wesley, whose theology has influenced to some degree forms of "Open and Relational Theology."

We begin with Edwards, the American Puritan theologian who believed that hell was an imminent threat to the unconverted, and

---

21. Tarald Rasmussen, "Hell Disarmed? The Function of Hell in Reformation Spirituality," *Numen* 56 (2009): 370-75.

22. Ignatius of Loyola, "The Spiritual Exercises," in *Ignatius of Loyaola: Spiritual Exercises and Selected Works (The Classics of Western Spirituality),* ed. George E. Ganss, S.J. (Mahwah, NJ: Paulist, 1991), 141-42.

therefore, it should be utilized with ferocity, both to warn the sheep and the unconverted. In his sermon "Sinners in the Hands of an Angry God" he emphasized God's power to throw the wicked into hell and that no one has the power to resist God. This is simply a matter of divine justice, for the wicked deserve their fate. Thus, the "wrath of God burns against them, their damnation does not slumber; the pit is prepared, the fire is made ready, the furnace is now hot, ready to receive them; the flames do now rage and glow."[23] One should not assume that this is not their fate.

Our final stop is Edwards' eighteenth-century English contemporary John Wesley. While Edwards was a Congregationalist and a Calvinist, Wesley was Anglican and Arminian. How they view predestination is not of first concern here as we are concerned about how Wesley understood the concept of hell. Wesley, like Edwards, believed that the fate of the wicked was eternal punishment in hell. That is, those who have made their place with the devil and his angels. In his "Great Assize" sermon on Romans 14:10, he connected the eternal nature of the punishment of the wicked to the eternal nature of the reward given to the righteous.[24] In his sermon "Of Hell," he spoke both of the horrors of eternal banishment from the presence of God and the fiery torment of those in Hell. Banishment is, in his mind, the equivalent of "eternal destruction." As for the fire of hell, it is not metaphorical. It is very much material and eternal in duration. He responds to the idea that since fire consumes, to be cast into the lake of fire one experiences annihilation. As did Augustine, so Wesley assumed that in the resurrection of the righteous and wicked, the resurrection body can be thrown in the fire and not be consumed, thus, the torment of hell is eternal.[25]

---

23. Jonathan Edwards, "Sinners in the Hands of an Angry God. A Sermon Preached at Enfield, July 8th, 1741" in *The Christian Theology Reader*, ed. Alister McGrath (Cambridge, MA: Blackwell, 1995), 361-62.

24. John Wesley, Sermon 15, "The Great Assize" *The Wesley Center Online. http://wesley. nnu.edu/john-wesley/the-sermons-of-john-wesley-1872-edition/sermon-15-the-great-assize/.

25. John Wesley, Sermon 73, "Of Hell" (October 10, 1782), *The Wesley Center Online. http:// wesley.nnu.edu/john-wesley/the-sermons-of-john-wesley-1872-edition/sermon-73-of-hell/.

Concluding Thoughts

I never imagined that I would attempt to write a history of the Christian doctrine of hell. I long ago dispensed with a belief in a literal place called hell in which God punished the wicked, though part of me has wondered what to do with people like Hitler and Stalin. The idea of hell is problematic, but it emerged as an answer to the problem of justice being fully served in this life. If justice is lacking in the here and now, then surely it will be completed in the afterlife. While some would accept death as the final answer to the problem of justice, for many that is not enough.

The concept of hell that has come down to us, which remains the majority position within Christianity, sought to answer the question of justice and create a sense of fear of what happens when we disobey God and embrace wickedness, which is embodied in the figure of Satan. The doctrine of hell has several points of origin. The most prominent being ancient Judaism (both the Old Testament and non-canonical texts) along with Greek philosophical and religious systems, including Plato. Jewish apocalypticism is an important contributor to early Christianity, as seen in such texts as the canonical Book of Daniel and the noncanonical First Enoch. As we've seen, these apocalyptic texts served as a response to Jewish experiences of conquest, persecution, and oppression. These works promised a beleaguered people both a promise of reward for faithfulness and punishment for the oppressor. These rewards and punishments would occur in the afterlife if not before. Ultimately, hell is an expression of the claim that vengeance belongs to God. That is the message Paul shares with the Roman church: "Beloved, never avenge yourselves, but leave room for the wrath of God, for it is written, "Vengeance is mine; I will repay, says the Lord" (Rom. 12:19; Deut. 32:35-36).

As we've seen in the course of this essay, it doesn't appear that Paul believed that divine judgment eventuated in eternal punishment. He appears to suggest that the fate of the wicked or unbeliever is death/annihilation. This was in keeping with early Jewish thinking. As early Christianity moved into the Greco-Roman world, it began to reframe Christian beliefs in line with Greek philosophical thinking, and that included the idea of an immortal soul. With that development, the idea of eternal punishment was a natural outcome. This development didn't move in just one direction. For example, Origen and those who followed him, including Gregory of Nyssa, could envision the restoration of all things (universal salvation). They might allow for a postmortem experience of purgation, but ultimately all would be restored. That is a view that I have found attractive. However, as we saw, especially in the western church, the majority position was expressed by Augustine and then further developed over time. In this view, divine judgment led to eternal punishment in a place known as hell. There were attempts to mitigate the problem of hell through the development of the idea of purgatory, but that middle option was dispensed with by the Reformers. Thus, for Protestants, the only options are heaven and hell unless you reject the majority position.

So, where does that leave those of us who find the concept of hell to be too problematic to embrace? How might we deconstruct hell and still affirm the importance of justice and take seriously the problem of evil in this world? How do we keep in tension God's judgment and God's love? It is easy to dispense with hell when one lives a comfortable, middle-class, suburban life (as I do). It's not so easy to dispense with it when one experiences oppression and sees no justice being served in life. If vengeance belongs to God as Deuteronomy and Paul suggest (Deut. 32:35; Rom. 12:19), then how does that take place? Resolving the problem of hell was not the task assigned to me.[26] My task is simply to provide a map that allows for a fruitful conversation. As for me, I place my hope in the promise that God will, in Christ, reconcile all things, and that my calling is to serve as an ambassador of that promise (2 Cor. 5:16-21). In my estimation that involves the restoration of all things, such that evil will be no more, and God will be "all in all" (1 Corinthians 15:28).

---

26. Dale Allison expresses well my own concerns about the problem of hell in *Night Comes: Death, Imagination, and the Last Things* (Grand Rapids, MI: Eerdmans, 2016), 93-119.

CHAPTER 2

The Philosophy of Eternal Life

R.T. Mullins

Abstract: The goal of this essay is to explore some options about eternal life from the perspective of open and relational theology. Though I don't fully fit into the open camp, I am deeply sympathetic to the views expressed by open and relational theology. In this essay, I will do my best to help you consider some different questions about eternal life from an open and relational perspective. To start our reflections, we first need to ask what kind of God we are considering when we are talking about open and relational theology. Then I will give special attention to God's love and moral goodness because that is important for understanding eternal life. The eternally loving God values friendship with humans, and thus offers humans an everlasting life. With this in mind, I will answer the question, "Are humans essentially eternal beings?" Answering this question leads me to my final set of questions for this essay. What is the quality of this everlasting life? Will some humans suffer forever, or will all be saved?

What Kind of God?

I take the concept of God to be that of a perfect being which is the single, ultimate foundation of reality. That is a fairly thin concept.

It does not really tell you much about God. What is interesting to consider are models of God. A model of God will give you a thicker description of what God is like. It will give you some unique claims about which attributes explain why God is perfect. A model of God will also fill out some details about what it means for God to be the foundation of reality. It is also worth pointing out that a model of God is not a complete systematic theology. A model of God is just one piece of a systematic theology. As I explain the different models of God, it will become clearer why open and relational theology is consistent with multiple models of God.

When it comes to God being perfect, there are certain divine attributes that are relatively uncontroversial. These are divine attributes that are widely agreed upon among the different models of God. They are important for understanding the nature of God, but they do not say anything particularly unique about God. These are attributes like necessary existence, aseity, eternality, omnipotence, omniscience, perfect goodness, perfect rationality, and perfect freedom. Necessary existence means that God cannot fail to exist. Aseity means that God's existence is not dependent upon, nor derived from anything external to God. Necessity and aseity entail that God is an eternal being. An eternal being exists without beginning and without end. I take omnipotence to be the most power-granting set of abilities, and no liabilities. One important power granting ability is cognitive perfection, which entails the ability to know all the facts about reality. In other words, omnipotence entails omniscience. Omnipotence also entails the power to perform free actions. Free actions are actions that agents intentionally perform for a reason. This leads to the next important power, which is the ability to be appropriately responsive to objective reasons. God is said to be perfectly rational in that God always acts for a reason. Lots of things can provide an agent with reasons to think, feel, and act in particular ways. One important set of reasons are moral values. Since God knows all the relevant moral values, and has the ability to be appropriately responsive to those values, God will always do what He has most objective reason to do.

When it comes to explaining how God is the foundation of reality, there are a few different options. For this essay, I will just focus on two popular views. These are creation *ex nihilo* and eternal creation. Creation *ex nihilo* says that there is some prior state of affairs where God exists all alone. You can call this the precreation moment. Some people think that this precreation moment is timeless, whilst others say that it is temporal. Yet everyone agrees that there is some precreation moment where God and God alone exists. In this precreation moment, God is free to create or not create. If God decides to create, He has a wide range of possible universes that He can bring about. Also, there is no material stuff from which God creates out of since God exists all alone. That is creation *ex nihilo*. Eternal creation disagrees. On a doctrine of eternal creation, God is never alone. God has always been creating a universe of some sort. God never exists without a universe of some sort. God is not free to create or refrain from creating, but God does have some discretion over which universe to bring about next. As I will explain shortly, models of God are divided over creation *ex nihilo*, eternal creation, and which kind of universe God created.

When it comes to distinguishing models of God, each model will make several unique claims about God's attributes. For example, classical theism says that there are four additional attributes that explain why God is perfect. Those are the attributes of timelessness, immutability, impassibility, and simplicity. Classical theism also says that God's maximal knowledge extends to the future because of the kind of universe that God has freely decided to create. Though seldom discussed, on classical theism, God's knowledge does not extend to the future because God essentially knows the future. There is no necessary or essential future on classical theism. On classical theism God is free to create a universe *ex nihilo*, or completely refrain from creating anything at all. The classical theist says that if God refrains from creating anything at all, then there is nothing for God to foreknow. What the classical theist is saying is that God has freely decided to create a universe that includes a settled future. On the basis of God's free decision to create a universe with a settled future, God has foreknowledge. Yet the classical theist faces an immediate difficulty when it comes to creation. She says that God is timeless and immutable, so God exists without succession and change. To put it mildly, it is incredibly difficult to understand how God can create a universe *ex nihilo* and not undergo change and succession. In a desperate attempt to avoid problems like these, classical theists have said that God is not really related to the universe! That is a remarkable claim, and open and relational theologians are quick to reject it.

Neoclassical theism is a somewhat messy model of God. I am a neoclassical theist, and I wish that the model were less messy, but such is life. The neoclassical theist denies one or more of the four classical attributes. She might reject timelessness and immutability in favor of temporality and mutability. She might reject impassibility in favor of passibility. She might reject simplicity in favor of unity. In previous publications, I have advocated for rejecting all four classical attributes.[1] I have no idea how many people I will convince of this. Neoclassical theism agrees with the classical theist about two things. First, she says that God's knowledge extends to the future because God has chosen to create a universe with a settled future. Second, God creates *ex nihilo*.

Open theism is a less messy model. Open theism says that God creates *ex nihilo*. Open theism denies all four of the classical attributes. Also, open theism says that God's knowledge does not extend to the future because God has freely chosen to create a universe with an open future. Exactly how history will unfold is not a settled matter.

Open theism quite obviously falls within the open and relational theology camp. The name itself is a pretty obvious give away. However, neoclassical theism can sometimes be allowed in the camp since neoclassical theists can affirm that God is genuinely related to the universe, and cares deeply for His creation. Especially if the neoclassical theist rejects all four of the classical attributes,

---

1. R. T. Mullins, *God and Emotion* (Cambridge: Cambridge University Press, 2020).

like I think she should. But there is one more model of God that is often associated with open and relational theology. This is called panentheism.

Much like neoclassical theism, panentheism is a messy model of God. Panentheism has a complicated history, and is often described using vague and meaningless metaphors stolen from classical theism. As a general rule of thumb, I do not recommend demarcating your model of God by using vague metaphors stolen from your rivals. Historically, most panentheists have affirmed the four classical divine attributes. Today, things are different. Many, but not all, panentheists reject the four classical attributes. Many, but not all, reject exhaustive divine foreknowledge. There is one thing that panentheists do seem to be united on today—eternal creation. Those panentheists who affirm open and relational theology reject exhaustive divine foreknowledge, reject the four classical attributes, and affirm eternal creation.

Deeper Reflections on Goodness and Love

You may have noticed that perfect love was not listed in the uncontroversial divine attributes. Personally, I think it ought to be uncontroversial, but I know too much about the history of Western philosophical theology to say that it is uncontroversial. Some classical theists argue that divine love adds nothing to our notion of divine goodness.[2] Other classical theists assert that all of God's love is self-love.[3] God only loves Himself, and in some convoluted way you might be able to metaphorically say that God loves you. This is utterly rejected by open and relational theology. Open and relational theology says that love is deeply important to a proper analysis of divine goodness, and that God deeply cares about His creatures.

---

2. Mark Murphy, *God's Own Ethics: Norms of Divine Agency and the Argument from Evil* (Oxford: Oxford University Press, 2017), 29-43.

3. Herman Bavinck, *The Doctrine of God* (Edinburgh: The Banner of Truth and Trust, 1979), 22.

The neoclassical theist Jordan Wessling has developed something called the *value account of love* that nicely captures a biblical account of divine love. It is the exact sort of thing that I believe open and relational theology needs in order to develop a robust account of divine love. Wessling tells us that love involves a trio of value.[4] What is love? Love is valuing a person's existence and flourishing, but it also involves valuing friendship with that person. When God loves someone, God deems it worthy that this person exist. He sees the value in that person existing. When God loves someone, God deems it worth pursuing the flourishing of that person. Why? Because God sees the value of that person's flourishing. When God loves someone, God deems it worth pursuing a friendship with that person. Why? Because God sees the value of a friendship with that person.

I think this connects nicely with a solid account of God's omniscience, goodness, and rationality. As perfectly rational, God will be appropriately responsive to reasons, and considerations of value are one kind of reason. God will always act for objectively good reasons that further His purposes. As perfectly good, God will always do what He has most objective reason to do, and will exhibit the most virtuous character when doing so. As omniscient, God will know what all the objective values that are worth responding to. On Wessling's analysis of love, human persons have great value. Since God is omniscient, God will know that human persons have great value. As perfectly good and rational, God will be appropriately responsive to the value of human persons.

This analysis of divine love also fits with the claim that God cares about His creatures. God sees that you have value and deems you to be worthy of His attention and action. In the philosophy of emotion, this is called caring or concern. Cares and concerns ground dispositions to have emotions and desires. If you care about something, you will be disposed to pay attention to it and to act

---

4. Jordan Wessling. *Love Divine: A Systematic Account of God's Love for Humanity.* (Oxford: Oxford University Press, 2020), 65.

on its behalf. Open and relational theology says that the Christlike God is one who cares deeply for His creation.

Are Humans Essentially Eternal Beings?

Often times, people will talk about the immortality of the soul. I think this is an unfortunately confused way of talking. Don't get me wrong, I firmly believe in the soul. I believe that I am an immaterial soul with a physical body. I also think that it is impossible to have life after death if I am not a soul. If I am identical to my body, then I see no possible way for me to survive the death of my body. With that being said, let me explain why the phrase "the immortality of the soul" is a bit confusing.

When we speak of the immortality of the soul, this often conjures up notions of the soul being essentially eternal and immortal. I think this is mistaken. Recall from above what it means to be eternal. To be eternal is to exist without beginning and without end. I don't know about you, but I began to exist. In fact, I think it is a safe bet that you began to exist as well. If that is right, you and I are not eternal.

As created beings, you and I are not necessarily existent either. God freely choose to create us. On neoclassical and open theism, God did not have to create anything at all. On the version of panentheism in view here, God did have to create something, but God has some discretion over what to create. All of these views entail that you and I did not have to exist. We are contingent beings.

This raises the question about life everlasting. Though you and I began to exist, we can potentially live forever. But there is a condition of course. There is always a catch, isn't there? The condition is God's sustaining activity. If God continues to sustain us in existence, then we can go on existing forever. If God does not choose to keep humans in existence, then *poof*, we are gone.

At this point, you are probably dying to know what happens after you die. Will God keep you in existence, or let you slip away into nothing? Some people think that God might allow certain individuals to cease to exist. Perhaps some people just don't want to be friends with God, so God lets them go *poof.* In the next section, I will consider this view further, and offer reasons for thinking that this is inconsistent with divine love. Since God values the existence and flourishing of humans, as well as values friendship with humans, it seems like a safe bet that God will sustain humans in existence forever.

Yet this raises another important question for the philosophy of eternal life. What is the quality of this everlasting life? There is a long line of thought within the history of Christianity that says the quality of this everlasting life will be great for some, but truly hellish for others. The claim is that some people will suffer forever. As I will explain in the next section, I think that open and relational theology should be skeptical about how hellish things can be in the afterlife.

Deconstructing Hell and the Quality of the Afterlife

We all want a good quality of life. If you are anything like me, you will also want a good quality of afterlife. I, for one, do not want to have an afterlife in hell where I am condemned to suffer forever and ever, amen! In light of God's perfect love, how should one think about the quality of the afterlife? In particular, how should one think about hell?

If you affirm an open and relational theology, or are at least flirting with it, you might be strongly tempted to deconstruct the notion that God will send people to hell to suffer forever. It is difficult to imagine how a loving God can value someone's flourishing, and condemn that person to an afterlife of everlasting suffering. I agree that this is difficult to imagine. However, I personally find myself with conflicting intuitions about the quality of the afterlife, and I am uncertain about how to properly rethink the doctrine of hell. This uncertainty should be expected since the process of deconstruction involves embracing uncertainty by considering new arguments and opposing views. What I will do in this final section is explain my uncertainty by exploring some different options and arguments about hell.

Start with a common gut reaction. In light of God's love, you might be tempted to say, "To hell with hell! There cannot be any hell if God is perfectly loving." I understand this gut reaction, but let me mention another gut reaction. In light of the atrocities of this world, you might be tempted to say, "To hell with all of you!" We all know of cases where certain people deserve to be punished for their wickedness. When I look at the world we live in, I strongly believe that certain people need to be punished for their atrocious sins. I see no obvious conflict between love and punishment here. After all, we often help people flourish by punishing them with an eye towards their repentance.

Where does that leave us? It might leave us with some justification to believe in some kind of notion of hell. Yet which doctrine of hell should one embrace? There are several different doctrines of hell floating around within the Christian tradition. I will discuss the four most popular. These are Eternal Conscious Torment, Possible Escape, Annihilationism, and Universalism. I will briefly describe each view, and explore some problems that arise for each view in light of love and open and relational theology. Yet before doing that, I need to explain where we are in the conversation. Thus far, I am saying that an open and relational theology will affirm the following.

1) The value account of divine love is true.

What I am about to do is ask you to consider different views on hell. It will be helpful to have some kind of criteria by which you can judge these different views. Here is the one that I suggest.

2) If a view on hell entails a divergence from one or more of the three values of love, then that is sufficient to reject that view.

So far so good. Everything here sounds in line with an open and relational theology. Now let me add a third assumption that I think Christians should be willing to accept because it is taught in scripture.

3) One day God will ultimately defeat evil.

Why should you affirm (3)? At least two reasons. First, the Bible says that God will one day ultimately defeat evil. (e.g. Revelation 20-22) Second, I think that a perfectly good God must punish wickedness, and bring about justice.

With this trio of assumptions, we can begin our exploration of different notions of hell. Here is this first inference I think that one can make from this trio of assumptions.

4) If God lets the damned carry on sinning forever in hell, then God will not ultimately defeat evil.

I take (4) to be obviously true. There cannot be an ultimate defeat of evil if there are a bunch of damned people in hell continuing to engage in a sinful rebellion against God. If that sin continues on forever and ever, God didn't do a very good job at defeating evil. A Christian cannot coherently say, "God ultimately defeated evil! Well, except for all those people over there in hell who are continuing to live in sinful rebellion against God." This leads me to make another inference. Given (3) and (4), I infer,

5) God does not let the damned carry on sinning forever in hell.

With premise (5), we reach in impasse. God does not let the damned carry on sinning forever in hell because God will ultimately defeat evil. How is God going to pull that off? Here is one option.

6) Eternal Conscious Torment: God ultimately defeats evil by sending the damned to face eternal conscious torment.

On this view, the damned suffer eternal conscious torment with no chance of relief. The suffering of the damned is not for their own good or flourishing. Also, the damned have no chance of entering into a right and loving friendship with God. The damned are sent to hell precisely to prevent their flourishing, and to prevent their friendship with God. On this view, the damned can no longer sin. Their fate is sealed, and they are no longer able to rebel or repent. They can do nothing but bear their just punishment for all of eternity. That is why evil is ultimately defeated on this view.

Eternal Conscious Torment gives us a clear defeat of evil, but you might be worried that it diverges from divine love. The divergence is not difficult to see. On this view of hell, the damned are prevented from flourishing and from having a friendship with God. That is a divergence from two of the three values of love. Given (2), one has sufficient grounds to reject this view of hell. So we need to look elsewhere to see how God can ultimately defeat evil without diverging from love. Here is another option.

7) Possible Escape: God sends people to hell in order to punish them, but in such a way that the damned have the opportunity to repent, reform, and enter heaven.

This is the position that Wessling endorses.[5] On this view, the damned are punished, but their fate is not eternally sealed. There is the opportunity to escape hell, but only if you repent and reform. This view is consistent with the three values of love. God values the damned's existence because He keeps them going. God also values their flourishing and friendship since He keeps providing them with opportunities to repent and reform. However, the problem is that (7) does not appear to be consistent with (3), the ultimate defeat of evil. On this view of hell, the damned have the option to repent or rebel. The reason anyone stays in hell is that they continue to reject God. The damned can potentially go on sinning forever

5. Ibid., 216.

by refusing to repent and reform. Even in hell, human persons can continue to sin, which is why there is no ultimate defeat of evil. That is a problem, so let's consider another option.

8) Annihilationism: God ultimately defeats evil by eradicating the damned from existence.

There are different versions of Annihilationism. On some views, God just eradicates an unrepentant sinner upon death. Others say that God will send a damned person to hell for a little while with no chance of escape. The damned will stay in hell for a while to receive punishment, and then will be eradicated from existence. Another version says that the damned are sent to hell for a while, and given the choice of annihilation or repentance.

I do not think that open and relational theology can accept this option since (8) conflicts with the value account of love. Notice that Annihilationism is a more extreme divergence than Eternal Conscious Torment. On Annihilationism, there is a divergence from all three values of love. First, God cannot be said to value the existence of a person if God eradicates her from existence. Second, God cannot be said to value the flourishing of a person if God eradicates her from existence. After all, a person cannot flourish if she does not exist. Third, God cannot be said to value friendship with a person if God eradicates her from existence. One usually does not put people in the friendzone by annihilating them from existence. I gather that if God annihilates you from existence, He is just not that into you. Hence, Annihilationism diverges from all three values of love. Given (2), there is sufficient reason to reject Annihilationism. So we need to look elsewhere to see how God can ultimately defeat evil without diverging from love.

The final view to consider is Universalism.

9) Universal Salvation: God ultimately defeats evil by bringing all to salvation.

Universalism does seem like the most obvious way for God to ultimately defeat evil at this point in the argument. On most accounts of Universalism, there are people who go to hell for a time. They are sent to hell until they repent and reform. The claim from the Universalist is that everyone will eventually repent and reform, and then enter into heaven. The human denizens of heaven will have freely cultivated a virtuous character such that it is no longer possible for them to sin. Hence, one day God will ultimately defeat evil.

That sounds promising, but I am uncertain if open and relational theology can really lead to Universalism. Here is why. Say God loves you, so God values your existence and flourishing, and values friendship with you. But also say that you are just a damned sinner, hell-bent on rejecting God's offer of friendship. God tells you to go to hell, and stay there until you clean up your act. God's punishment in this case is intended to reform you. God keeps you in existence, and performs actions that will hopefully lead to your eventual flourishing, and hopefully lead to a great friendship with God. But God gave you free will, and it is logically impossible for God to control your free actions. So there can be no guarantee that you will ever clean up your act. You could potentially persist in your sinful rebellion forever. If God created an open universe and does not know exactly how the future will unfold, not even God could know if you will ever repent. Hence, no clear cut universal salvation. At best, there can only be a hope that universal salvation will obtain. That leaves me uncertain about Universalism.

It is certainly the case that many open and relational theologians strongly lean towards Universalism.[6] They find arguments like mine against the other views quite persuasive, and thus embrace Universalism. Yet I find myself uncertain how open and relational theology can be confident in this. Open and relational

---

6. Thomas Jay Oord. *Open and Relational Theology: An Introduction to Life Changing Ideas.* New York: SacraSage Press 2021, 112-13.

theologians often say that God takes a legitimate risk when He creates a universe. The very real risk is that certain human persons will reject God's offer of friendship. Many open and relational theologians claim that God cannot guarantee that His plan to enter into friendship with all human persons will succeed. If they are correct, then I do not understand how any open and relational theologian can be confident in Universalism or God's ultimate defeat of evil. Both of those seem like serious problems. Of course, I have elsewhere argued that open and relational theologians have greatly exaggerated the risks that God takes when God creates a universe.[7] If I am right about this, then open and relational theologians will need to rethink a few things beyond deconstructing the doctrine of hell. Thankfully for you my dear reader, this book contains essays that aim to develop plausible alternative views from an open and relational perspective. That is theology in action!

I think that this further exploration of open and relational theology is a good thing. Rethinking one's faith is difficult, but worth it. We are all trying to better understand God and the world we live in. I ask that we help each other rethink our faith with charity and grace as we hope for the completion of God's plan.

---

7. R.T. Mullins. *Divine Temporality and Providential Bodgery*. Theologica 5 (2021), 147-74; R.T. Mullins and Emanuela Sani. *Open Theism and Risk Management: A Philosophical Biological Perspective*. Zygon 56 (2021), 591-613

CHAPTER 3

Divine Injustice: The Problem of Hell

Julie Ferwerda

Back in the day, when I was a full-fledged believer in the doctrine of hell, as in *eternal torment and separation from God*, I never stopped to consider the implications of this belief from the standpoint of God's character and objective justice. Is the notion of eternal punishment consistent with God's character? Could a "loving God" justly punish most of his children for 50 billion years in exchange for a finite number of sins and failures in a mortal lifetime? Would a reality of hell ultimately reveal God's character to be benevolent or malevolent? A loving parent or a psychopath torturer? It's time to examine this long-held orthodox Christian teaching in light of the character and purposes of God.

Mean or weak God

If such a place as hell exists, it ultimately implies that God is either too callous and mean-hearted to devise a plan where he values, chooses, and saves the masses of unbelievers, or else too weak or disinterested to overcome the free will of the same masses in order to save them. These two diametrically opposed views, held and taught by intelligent, seminary-trained theologians, pastors, and

Bible teachers, encompass the doctrinal beliefs of nearly one hundred percent of conservative Christians worldwide.

Calvinism declares that God is *unwilling*—does not desire—to save all of His children because He has only "elected" a few for salvation. This theological sway says that God purposely created most of His own children to be damned forever, perhaps merely to provide a contrast to those whom He created to love forever. *Arminianism,* on the other hand, declares that God *desires* but is unable to save all people because He cannot infringe upon the "free will" of humans, even that of uninformed, blind, deceived, inherently self-destructive beings.

These two tenets attempt to interpret the Bible on what I consider to be two of the most important foundation stones of the entire Christian faith—who is worthy for salvation, and whose will prevails in the end—man's or God's? We will address these questions, but first let us consider the implications of these two doctrinal positions and their ultimately flawed reasoning in light of the destiny of billions of humans.

In either of these models, God is all-powerful *until* one gets to the problem of evil and/or the obstacle of human will. These two forces are supposedly able to usurp God's ultimate power, will, and control over His creation. The hardness of the human heart and the power of free will are more prevailing and determinate than God's loving heart and will. Creation appears to be spinning out of control and all God can do is to stand back with His hands tied, putting out fires and hoping He can salvage a little something before the end. At last, He will be able to save a precious few while containing the rest of all that evil in hell.

Depending on which doctrine you adhere to, the Kingdom of God appears to be either an anarchy or a dictatorship, yet they can't both be right. Shouldn't there be solid, conclusive evidence for only one "right" position on so crucial a matter? *More importantly, is there a chance they could both be wrong?* Could this polarizing dichotomy merely be a distraction from a much greater deception, leading us away from *the problem of hell,* as it relates to divine justice? Let us consider the implications of hell from a moral standpoint where it sabotages the character and trustworthiness of God.

Inconsistent and Double-Minded

Believing in hell takes a lot of faith. The Scriptural and historical evidence for such a place is suspiciously missing as the supposed destination for most of humanity.[1] It is also curious how hard most Christians have to work at ignoring all the parts of Scripture they don't want to acknowledge, while putting a death grip on the parts they do want to see and believe. If taken literally, it appears that God condemns most with a hard line of no return, while bending the rules or providing special favor to others, resulting in an uneven, unfair playing field for humanity. Being "saved" in the traditional sense appears more like an ultra-exclusive club. In this private club model, God personally takes credit for choosing a precious few while hiding the truth from the rest of the "outsiders."

So, who can actually qualify for the club membership? If we are going to give equal weight to all passages, not disregarding the ones that don't conveniently fit in with our current belief system, a lot more people must actually be going to hell than once thought.

Orphans. It is estimated that there are 150 million orphans in our world today, not to mention widows, lepers, and other destitute. Orthodoxy says that most of these hopeless children are doomed if they don't say the sinner's prayer and put their faith in Jesus before they die. Yet one who believes in this outcome should find it strange that, though God frequently speaks of assisting orphans and widows throughout His Word, He almost exclusively exhorts His followers to defend their rights and feed them (James 1:27). Never once does He say to share the Gospel with them or snatch them from eternal flames.

---

1. For an in-depth deconstruction of the doctrine of hell refer to my book, *Raising Hell: Christianity's Most Controversial Doctrine Put Under Fire,* available for free at www.raising-hellbook.com or on Amazon.

If God were planning to send most of the world's poorest of the poor to hell because they don't believe in Him (or they aren't "chosen"), why would He care about meeting their physical needs while they're alive? I don't see what difference it would make for these outcasts to have a few extra years of full stomachs while living in a "hell on earth" in every other way. We'd basically be prolonging their suffering and giving them a little pat on the back before sending them off to everlasting doom.

Masses. Have you ever noticed that when Jesus spoke to the general crowds, He always set up mental obstacles by teaching exclusively with parables (Matt. 13:34)? The disciples, His closest companions, complained that the parables were difficult to understand, asking for insight. Why would Jesus make life-saving truth so obscure? According to Jesus in Mark 4:10–12. "…His followers, along with the twelve, began asking Him about the parables. And He was saying to them, 'To you (disciples) has been given the mystery of the kingdom of God, but those who are outside get everything in parables, so that while seeing, they may see and not perceive, and while hearing, they may hear and not understand, otherwise they might return and be forgiven.'"

Unless you're a Calvinist and you've already made your peace with such a heinous outcome for poor unsuspecting outsiders, you have to admit that it's unconscionable for the "Savior" to actually hide the truth from the crowds—truth which supposedly would have kept them out of hell. He apparently intentionally doomed those crowds of people forever without any real chance at belief. Not only does that realization fail to correspond with the forgiving and loving nature of God as revealed in Scripture, but also it sounds vindictive.

Wise and learned. Jesus said. "I praise You, O Father, Lord of heaven and earth, that You have hidden these things from the wise and intelligent and have revealed them to infants" (Luke 10:21–24). If Jesus rejoiced about God hiding truth from educated and intelligent teachers and religious hierarchy from his own heritage, does that mean He was glad they were going to hell? Wouldn't this truth also apply to educated and intelligent religious leaders today?

Disobedient people. Jesus frequently made statements like: "Not everyone who says to Me, 'Lord, Lord,' will enter the kingdom of heaven, but he who does the will of My Father will enter'" (Matt. 7:21). Paul, the apostle to the Gentiles, made many similar statements to *believing* Jews and Gentiles alike, warning them of missing out on the promises of the future Sabbath Rest due to disobedience (see Heb. 4:1, 11). Does this mean all disobedient Christians are going to hell?

Rich people. I wonder how wealthy one has to be in order to qualify. I once read that a new mega-church, presumably funded by comfortably wealthy churchgoers, opens every few days in the U.S.[2] One went up in Dallas a few years ago for 120 million dollars. Yet statistics tell us that only two percent of American church budgets go to overseas missions and humanitarian aid, while more than thirty percent or more go exclusively to building projects.[3] The warning written to *believers* in James 5:1–5 feels applicable here: "Come now, you rich, weep and howl for your miseries which are coming upon you. …Your gold and your silver have rusted, and…will be a witness against you and will consume your flesh like fire."

Gentiles. In the days of Jesus, it appears that all the Gentiles (non-Jews) went to hell due to ignorance of the Hebrew God: "These twelve Jesus sent out after instructing them: 'Do not go in the way of the Gentiles, and do not enter any city of the Samaritans…'" (see Matt. 10:5–6; 15:22–24). If Jesus knew the Gentiles of His

2. William C. Symonds, "Earthly Empires: How Evangelical Churches are Borrowing from the Business Playbook," *Business Week*, May 23, 2005, http://www.businessweek.com/magazine/content/05_21/b3934001_mz 001.htm.

3. Jared Brian, "Church Stewardship & Tithing Report," Tithing.com, accessed June 28, 2010, http://churchtithesandofferings.com/blog/giving-statistics.

day were headed into the horrors of hell, how could He possibly ignore them?

Jews. After the days of Jesus, when the Gentiles finally got included in the plan of salvation, it appears that there was a big shift and all the Jews started going to hell. "God gave them (Jews) a spirit of stupor, eyes to see not and ears to hear not, down to this very day... Let their table become a snare and a trap, and a stumbling block and a retribution to them. Let their eyes be darkened to see not, and bend their backs forever" (Romans 11:7–10).

If we are to consider and apply all passages equally and fairly from our modern Bible translations, who is left for the Kingdom? Maybe a few missionaries who gave up everything to follow Jesus? Mother Teresa, assuming she actually said the sinner's prayer before she died? Perhaps children who have not yet reached "the age of accountability"? Unless there's an alternative to what we've always been taught, the odds don't look good for most of us.

Unfair

The Christianity I was raised with declares that unless someone says the "sinner's prayer" and "accepts Jesus as their Lord and Savior" before they die, they are going to hell. In this worldview, *multiple billions of people are doomed* without a fair chance, because one's opportunity to be saved is most directly related to the geographic location, family, and religion into which they were born.

Most Christians would probably object to comparing Christianity to a club membership, stating that anyone can join. But can anyone really join if they don't know the club exists, or would most people even want to join if they were told, "join this club or burn forever in hell"?

And what about those who are mentally, physically, or psychologically handicapped? What about the countless poverty-stricken people who have historically scrounged to survive? And what do we do with all those millions of people who lived before Jesus? How about the billions who have been raised devout followers of their religions and that's all they've ever known? Are they going to be faulted for "rejecting" Him?

When pressed about the unfairness of such a deity, many pastors and teachers say that if no one reaches these people with the gospel, that God somehow reveals himself to all these billions of souls so that they are "without excuse" for rejecting him. *Really?* Then why send missionaries?

Satan Wins and God Loses

Pause to think about a god who would torture people 30 trillion years for mistakes made over a few decades. His feeble, fallible hopes for His own children are dependent upon human free will, and confined to the length of one's brief, mortal lifespan. Sadly, this fabricated god is more like Hitler than Mother Teresa.

As a result, orthodox Christianity would have you believe that billions of people are headed toward everlasting separation from God because Satan successfully deceived them in a cosmic tug-of-war. Hence, God is forced to drop his end of the rope, turning most of his creation over to unstoppable evil in an unsafe, overwhelmingly dark universe. God must also concede that most of His children are nothing more than throwaways who are not worth fighting for.

Set Up for Failure

Too many people try to divorce God's unconditional, "unfailing" love from His justice. Sure, intentional wrongs demand a judicial process. But tell me, how could torturing someone endlessly, even for the most grievous behaviors over a mortal lifetime, be considered equitable? True and perfect justice demands a loving, restorative remedy for all sin because we were all born into this realm with the propensity to do harm. Mankind was basically set up for utter failure, perhaps in order to learn what can be learned no other way. Paul plainly states in Romans 11:32: "For God has shut up all in disobedience so that He may show mercy to all." Apparently, the same "all" who have been locked up in disobedience, with no choice about it, will be shown mercy.

Many churches today teach that the fall of Adam and Eve was basically "Plan B." Adam and Eve, they say, were created perfect, were intended to stay perfect, and God was merely doing "damage control" by setting in motion a solution for their unexpected sin. But if Plan B is even possible, and God did not fully plan out and expect what went down in the Garden ahead of time, and if God threw His hands up helplessly because of man's "free will," what's to keep His creation from necessitating a Plan C, or a Plan D? If God really must work around the supposed free will of humans, what's to keep man from messing up the plan continuously?

Adam and Eve did not mess up Plan A. The fall into the forgetfulness and perception of separation from God and others (and behaviors that result) was Plan A all along. There's a God-made law in the Torah that sums up Plan A, whereby God takes responsibility for the fallen state of His own creation: "If a man digs a pit and does not cover it over, and an ox or a donkey falls into it, the owner of the pit shall make restitution" (Exod. 21:33–34). In his book *Free Will Versus Ownership,* Stephen Jones explains:

"God is both the owner of the pit and the owner of the ox (Adam). First, God dug a pit, because He created an opportunity for Adam to sin. ...That made God legally liable by His own law and created a 'tension' that demanded a resolution. ...The fact is that God knew the end from the beginning. He was not taken by surprise. He dug that pit and left it uncovered because He had a plan, and the plan called for man to fall. By God's own liability laws, then, He is responsible. So what did God do about it? He sent His only begotten Son who was lifted up on the cross in order to drag all men to Himself (John 12:32). ...The ox is now His."[4]

---

4. Stephen E. Jones, *Free Will Versus Ownership* (Fridley, MN: God's Kingdom Ministries, 2007) https://godskingdom.org/studies/books/free-will-versus-ownership.

The Reality of a Loving Supreme God

If God is better than we've been indoctrinated to believe, where do we start to heal the wound? How do we begin to understand his plan for all his beloved offspring—even the "bad" ones? Let us turn to the best example available to help us discern a truer picture of God's character—functional, stable, loving parents! If God is the ultimate Parent, and his ways are higher than our ways, there is no possible outcome in this Story where earthly parents would be able to outperform God in the ways of love and grace toward their children.

Loving parents only intend good for their children. No good parent ever sets out to harm their children. On the contrary! Our kids may see our discipline that way, but ultimately everything we do is with the intent of helping them become successful, contributing members of society with the ability to nurture loving relationships throughout their lives. Could God's intent be any less for His children? In his 1843 book, *The Plain Guide to Universalism,* Thomas Whittemore wrote, "[God] would not have created intelligent beings, had He known they were to be forever miserable. To suppose that God would bring beings into existence, who He knew would be infinite losers by that existence, is to charge Him with the utmost malignity. The existence itself would not be a blessing, but a curse; the greatness of which cannot be described."[5]

Loving parents make sure the punishment fits the crime. Can you imagine locking your children up in a dungeon and then punishing them for the rest of their lives for an act (or season) of rebellion? One little-understood intent of the Levitical Law, "an eye for an eye and a tooth for a tooth," (lex talionis) is the underlying admonition to not over-punish the offender, while at the same time providing a way of restoration back into the community.

---

5. Thomas Whittemore, *The Plain Guide to Universalism* (Boston: Whittemore, 1843).

Loving parents understand underlying reasons behind disobedience. Frequently you hear parents of toddlers defending their ill behavior. A good parent, knowing their child intimately, is able to offer patient understanding when the need arises. As this same child grows up, life often inflicts wounds and scars on his or her heart. Good parents know that there are factors that contribute to why their children do the things they do—physical pain, exhaustion, sin or dysfunction of those around them, emotional hurts and scars, injuries caused by others, disabilities, genetic disorders, chemical imbalances, and disappointments of life. How much more must God understand why His children act the way they do and plan ways to help them overcome?

It's easy to assume that we all have a choice to "be good," especially if we have grown up in a loving home with little pain and suffering. But many of us have never tasted the hard life. Many of us have never been severely mistreated, abandoned, abused, or exploited. How could we not expect and believe that the heavenly Parent understands the deception of and resulting rebellion by His children who are offered little love or kindness during their mortal lives? How could we be so narrow-minded and unloving to judge that any of these people "chose this path" or "deserve what they get?" Even God's seemingly hardened and rebellious children are treated with patience. "He will not always strive with us, nor will He keep His anger forever. He has not dealt with us according to our sins, nor rewarded us according to our iniquities" (Psalm 103:9–10).

Loving parents demonstrate fair and consistent character. Suppose you had a set of parents who had four children. For whatever reason (rebellion, disobedience, or personality conflict) the parents locked one of the children in the basement where they isolated and punished the child excessively. Do you think the other children in the home could (or should) trust parents who would do this to "one of them"?

As I consider how Christianity is portrayed to the world, is this not the malevolent image we have unwittingly pinned on God? Is this perhaps the reason many people are atheistic or distrustful of a "god like that" and why many violent atrocities have been done in God's name?

Loving parents ultimately long to be restored in relationship. Every loving parent longs to be reconciled to a wayward child. The focus of Levitical Law was to teach people that *reconciliation* is the satisfaction (atonement) for sin and broken relationships, not destruction or casting away. The intent of the Torah was to compensate the one injured *and* to restore the offender to society.

It is true that sometimes as parents we have to take a heavy hand with our children, causing pain or separation of relationship for a time. Ultimately however, our deepest desire is to weed out rebellion. Sometimes a short-term separation or conflict is worth the end result—a child who learns a valuable lesson through hardship, who does not want to repeat that behavior, and who comes to us in humility, realizing the error of his or her ways and desiring a restored relationship. This is the sentiment behind the parable of the Prodigal Son in Luke 15.

Loving parents never give up. It's double-minded to tell the world that God loves them unconditionally, yet if they don't pray a certain prayer before they die, His love becomes conditional and temporary. Interview any loving parents and you will not find one that would give up on their children—ever. How then could we believe that the OG Parent would ever give up on even one of His children?

Truly loving parents demonstrate trustworthiness, fairness, and consistency with all their children, creating a sense of fearlessness and security that leads to thriving in the home. And if the children are to emulate these kinds of parents, such behavior breeds peace, acceptance, and unconditional love among the whole family.

God's Perfect Will

We are left with the questions: Who is worthy for salvation, and whose will prevails, man's or Gods? What is God's will and plan for humanity—even the seemingly lost souls?

An interesting word study in the Greek reveals that the word *thelema* translated God's "will," is a very strong word declaring that God fully expects to accomplish his intention and plan for creation—there is no other outcome. "My plan will be established, and I will accomplish all My good pleasure…truly I have spoken; truly I will bring it to pass. I have planned *it*, I will certainly do it" (Isaiah 46:10-11). What Does God Will? What does God want? He's made it clear throughout Scripture:

> *God wills that not one should perish or be lost (John 3:35; 6:39; 2 Peter 3:9, KJV).

> *God wills all people to be saved (1 Tim. 2:3–4, KJV).

> *God wills that His will should be done by all (Matt. 6:10; Dan. 2:35).

> *God has declared that every knee will bow to Him, and every tongue will confess Him as Lord while giving Him praise (Rom. 14:11, Phil. 2:10).

Who is Valued?

All humanity is God's offspring (Col. 1:15). That's right. You don't have to be a Christian to be one of God's children, as Paul explained to the Greek idol worshipers in Acts 17. Just as our children are physiologically the sum total of the genetic codes we have passed onto them, we each possess the spiritual DNA of our heavenly Father. In order for His nature to be fully expressed and for creation to be perfectly restored, all of these divinely patterned expressions of Him must be gathered back to Him in perfect unity of purpose, yet each retaining unique individuality.

The Scriptures describe God as a "consuming fire." Ancient Hebrew teachings describe all people as "divine sparks" out of that Fire, expressing His vitality and passion in the world. This is why people everywhere are inspired, unique, and magnificent reflections of the Divine through our gifts, dreams, talents, and desires. Through each of us is revealed a different aspect of the God-nature. For Him to lose even one of those sparks would mean He loses an aspect of Himself.

Is it not the same with our own children, each their own yet fully out of us? When I consider the bond that earthly parents have with their children, I know it's utterly impossible that God would ever ask us to lose a part of ourselves forever—any more than He would ever give up a part of Himself. His answer is not damnation, but regeneration and healing.

A true father's love cannot be earned, and it cannot be done away with. Just as we would never give up on our children, God will never give up on His children; His love will not fail us.

In closing, I leave you with a quote by Hannah Whitall Smith from her 1904 book, *The Unselfishness of God: My Spiritual Autobiography.* [6] "But now I began to see that the wideness of God's love was far beyond any wideness that I could even conceive of; and that if I took all the unselfish love of every mother's heart the whole world over, and piled it all together, and multiplied it by millions, I would still only get a faint idea of the unselfishness of God.

"...Most of my ideas of the love and goodness of God have come from my own experience as a mother, because I could not conceive that God would create me with a greater capacity for unselfishness and self-sacrifice than He possessed Himself... Since I had this insight of the mother-heart of God, I have never been able

---

6. To read the three chapters edited out of Hannah's original book, go to: www.tentmaker. org/books/unselfishness-of-god.htm.

to feel the slightest anxiety for any of His children; and by His children I do not mean only the good ones, but I mean the bad ones just as much. I had, in short, such an overwhelming revelation of the intrinsic and inherent goodness and unselfishness of God that nothing since has been able to shake it."[7]

---

7. Hannah Whitall Smith, *The Unselfishness of God: My Spiritual Autobiography* (Littlebrook, 1988).

CHAPTER 4

Constructing a Biblical Theology of Hell: The Case for Universal Restoration

Keith Giles

The doctrine of Universal Reconciliation, or Apokatastasis, is entirely Biblical. In other words, the belief itself is rooted completely in the teachings of the Old Testament prophets, the Apostles of the New Testament scriptures, and, of course, Jesus himself.

This may come as a shock to many who have never studied the doctrine very closely, especially for those who have simply accepted the rhetoric often repeated from the pulpit that "No one ever spoke about Hell more than Jesus did" or that "the Scriptures clearly teach that those who reject Christ will spend an eternity in Hell," etc.

Not only are these sorts of claims false and misleading, they are inconsistent with what we see reflected in the scriptures regarding God's reaction to sin, God's character and nature as revealed by Christ, and the explicit teachings from both Jesus and the Apostle Paul concerning the purpose of God's discipline and the goal of God's ultimate plans for those created in God's own image.

This short chapter will endeavor to illuminate some of the more prominent scriptures concerning these points, but unfortunately, we won't have the space here to cover all the verses that support the doctrine of Universal Reconciliation. So far, I have found over 76 verses in the Scriptures that support the notion of ultimate redemption for all humanity, for example. Therefore, we will do our best to highlight the most relevant texts in the space we have available to us in this volume.[1]

From a purely Biblical perspective, what we see in the Hebrew Scriptures, commonly referred to as the Old Testament, is absolute silence on the subject of Eternal Torment. Simply put, the Jewish texts say nothing whatsoever about anyone suffering an eternity in the flames of Hell as punishment for their sins or for rejecting the testimony of God.

What we do find, however, are verses that expound upon the lovingkindness of God that "endures forever,"[2] and the favor of God that "is everlasting,"[3] and promises that God's desire is to prepare "for all people a feast"[4] and to "swallow up death forever"[5] and that "all the nations of the earth shall be blessed,"[6] and that "every knee shall bow"[7] and that "all mankind shall come and swear an oath of allegiance to God,"[8] etc.

What's more, we find specific verses that declare God's promise "not to take away a life [and to] devise plans so that the one banished from Him does not remain banished." (2 Sam. 14:14)

We also find dozens of verses in those Old Testament scriptures which affirm, over and over again, that, in the end, "all the earth shall worship [God] and sing praises"[9], and that "The Lord will

---

1. My book, *Jesus Undefeated: Condemning the False Doctrine of Eternal Torment* (Quoir, 2019), covers most of the texts supporting Universal Reconciliation, in addition to providing an appendix of those 76 verses alluded to here.

2. Ps. 136:1-6

3. Ps. 30:4-5

4. Isa. 25:6-8

5. Ibid.

6. Gen. 18:18; 12:3; 28:14

7. Isa. 45:21-25

8. Ibid.

9. Ps. 66:3-4

not cast off forever...yet will show compassion according to the multitudes of His mercies."[10]

Of course, the greatest scriptural source for the doctrine of Universal Reconciliation comes from the New Testament scriptures, and so that is where we will focus our attention now.

When some Christians read the red letters of the Gospels where Jesus speaks of "coming judgment" and "the place where the worm does not die and the fire is not quenched"[11], or speaks of the unrighteous as being sent away "into outer darkness"[12] or to be cast "into everlasting fire prepared for the devil and his angels,"[13] they wrongly assume that Jesus is speaking of where anyone goes after they die, and they miss the fact that, in every case, he is quoting Old Testament prophets who were using a common Jewish teaching style known as "Apocalyptic Hyperbole."

As we've already shown, those Old Testament prophets never spoke once about anything resembling the doctrine of Eternal Conscious Torment. So, when Jesus uses language that echoes the words of Isaiah, or Jeremiah, or the other prophets, he is not speaking of what happens to anyone after they die. He is quoting those prophets and using that language to say exactly what they were saying: that a very real destruction was inevitable unless the people changed their behavior and listened to the warnings of the prophet.

So, when Isaiah warned Egypt (in Isaiah 19:1) that they would see the Lord God "riding on a swift cloud" and "coming to Egypt", it wasn't a literal statement. God did not actually mount a cloud pony and ride in the sky above Egypt. But, what did happen was that invading armies came against them and defeated them and took many of them as captives.

---

10. Lam. 3:31-32

11. Mark 9:48

12. Matt. 22:13

13. Matt. 25:41

When Jesus quotes Isaiah 66:24 (in Mark 9:43-48) and warns the people of his day about avoiding the fate where "the worm does not die and the fire is not quenched", they knew what he meant. They understood that by quoting the passage in Isaiah, Jesus was speaking of the exact same sort of judgment that would take place, not in some spiritual reality after they were dead, but in their own lifetime.

In fact, that passage where Jesus quotes Isaiah is actually speaking of those who would "go out and look on the dead bodies of the men who rebelled against [God]". So, those who rebelled are dead. They are not suffering torment. The fires are not quenched because—using hyperbole—the number of bodies is nearly endless, and the worm does not die because, once again, the source of food they consume in terms of dead bodies is practically without end.

What's more, the place where those dead bodies are thrown is literally, in the Greek, *Gehenna*, which is not an eternal spiritual place of suffering but a very real, literal valley (Hinnom) just outside the walls of Jerusalem.

Once you understand Jesus's use of Apocalyptic Hyperbole in the Gospels, these supposed references to eternal punishment can be more easily understood as references to real-world suffering at the hands of invading armies in response to the people's lack of repentance.

The fulfillment of those warnings came, just as Jesus predicted, within the lifetime of his listeners—roughly 40 years later—when the Roman armies surrounded Jerusalem in 70 AD and destroyed the Jewish Temple, brought an end to the daily sacrifices, and brought about the "end of the age" (not the end of the world).[14]

So, if Jesus never actively taught the doctrine of Endless Torment, does that necessarily mean that he taught the doctrine of Universal Reconciliation?

---

14. A more extensive exploration of Apocalyptic Hyperbole can be found in my books *Jesus Unexpected: Ending the End Times to Become the Second Coming* (Quoir, 2020), and *Jesus Undefeated: Condemning the False Doctrine of Eternal Torment* (Quoir, 2019).

Let's see if we can find evidence of ultimate reconciliation in the teachings of Christ.

When we examine the teachings of Jesus, what we find is quite startling, especially in terms of how he approaches the notions of forgiveness, judgement and mercy.

When Jesus suggests that "if you've seen me, you've seen the Father" (John 14:9), the implication is clear: If you want to know what God is really like, look at Jesus. So, when we look at Jesus what we see is a God who forgives everyone, all the time, instantly, without waiting for anyone to confess or repent or even ask for forgiveness. Jesus always declares "your sins are forgiven" to everyone who comes to him seeking to be healed or restored.

As New Testament scholar and author, David Bentley Hart observes:

> *"If it is from Christ that we are to learn how God relates himself to sin, suffering, evil, and death, it would seem that he provides us little evidence of anything other than a regal, relentless, and miraculous enmity; sin he forgives, suffering he heals, evil he casts out, and death he conquers. And absolutely nowhere does Christ act as if any of these things are part of the eternal work or purposes of God."*[15]

Jesus also declares in the Gospel of John, chapter 12, verse 32 that his mission is to literally drag (*helkuo* in the Greek), "all mankind to [Himself]"

In the Gospel of John, we also find two quite shocking statements from Jesus where he says:

> *"Moreover, the Father judges no one, but has entrusted all judgment to the Son.." (John 5:2)*

15. David Bentley Hart, *The Doors of the Sea: Where Was God in the Tsunami?* (Grand Rapids, MI: Eerdmans, 2005), 86-87.

And then surprisingly adds, a few chapters later, this startling admission:

"I pass judgment on no one." (John 8:15)

So, if the Father judges no one but leaves that to the Son, and if the Son says, "I judge no one," where does that leave us? What are we to do with passages where Jesus famously speaks about the separation of the sheep and the goats in Matthew 25: 41-46?:

Then he will say to those on his left, **'Depart from me, you cursed, into the eternal fire prepared for the devil and his angels.** *For I was hungry and you gave me no food, I was thirsty and you gave me no drink, I was a stranger and you did not welcome me, naked and you did not clothe me, sick and in prison and you did not visit me.' Then they also will answer, saying, 'Lord, when did we see you hungry or thirsty or a stranger or naked or sick or in prison, and did not minister to you?' Then he will answer them, saying, 'Truly, I say to you, as you did not do it to one of the least of these, you did not do it to me.'* **And these will go away into eternal punishment, but the righteous into eternal life.** *(emphasis mine)*

This passage is probably the most often quoted by those who argue for Eternal Torment since it appears that Jesus equates the eternal quality of those being punished with the eternal duration of those being rewarded. We can't say the punishment isn't eternal without suggesting that the eternal life experienced by the righteous isn't also without end. Or can we?

The word "eternal" used twice in this passage is the Greek word *aionios* and while it may often be used to suggest an endless duration of time, it is also quite frequently used in the scriptures to describe events that are not endless but merely "a very long time."

For example, in the Greek translation of the Old Testament scriptures, the Hebrew word *olam* is translated into the Greek word *aionios* in Isaiah 32:14-15 which says:

> *"**The fortress will be abandoned, the noisy city deserted;
> citadel and watchtower will become a wasteland forever**
> (aionios), the delight of donkeys, a pasture for flocks, **until
> the Spirit is poured on us from on high, and the desert
> becomes a fertile field, and the fertile field seems like a
> forest.**"* (emphasis mine)

Notice that while the fortress is prophesied to become an "abandoned...wasteland forever" (using the Greek word *aionios*), that will last "until the Spirit is poured out on us", which would mean it wouldn't actually remain that way "forever" but merely "a very long time."

There are numerous other examples of this term *aionios* being used in this same way; to describe an event as lasting "almost forever" but literally so.

The same is true for the Hebrew word *olam,* which is also used over 300 times in the Old Testament scriptures to indicate something that endures for a very long time, but not necessarily without end. In at least twenty cases, the word *olam* is used to refer to events in the past. Therefore, *olam* and *aionios* are quite often used to refer to events that last a very long time, but are not necessarily without end.

Even someone like Francis Chan, who holds to the doctrine of Eternal Torment, admits in his book on this subject, *Erasing Hell,* that his confidence in the word *aionios* as a reference to something that is literally endless was shaken once he realized how often the term was used to describe events that were not always endless, saying:

> *"The debate about hell's duration is much more complex than
> I first assumed. While I lean heavily on the side that says it*

is everlasting, I am not ready to claim that with complete certainty."[16]

However, even if the term *aionios* was intended to suggest an endless quality of the fire in the Matthew 25 passage, we need to understand the nature of the fire as a metaphor for purification and restoration throughout the scriptures.

Many of us have so conditioned to read verses that speak of people being "thrown into the lake of fire" or subjected to "the eternal fire" of judgment, that we assume this must indicate either a state of endless suffering and torture, or the place where sinners are consumed and annihilated by God.

But, is that the way this metaphor of God's fire is used in the Hebrew scriptures, or in the New Testament? Not at all.

What we see in the Old Testament is the idea that God is "a consuming fire" that burns away our impurities and refines us into the original image of God found within every single one of us.

For example, in Malachi 3:2, when speaking of the great and terrible Day of the Lord where God comes to render a final judgment on the earth, here is what we find:

> *"But who can endure the day of his coming? Who can stand when he appears? **For he will be like a refiner's fire or a launderer's soap.**"*

The fire metaphor is equated with the quality of soap which does not destroy or torture, but which makes us pure and clean.

This is especially comforting when we read Jesus uttering words like this:

> *"For everyone will be salted with fire."* (Mark 9:47-49)

---

16. Francis Chan and Preston M. Sprinkle, *Erasing Hell: What God Said about Eternity, and the Things We've Made Up* (Colorado Springs, CO: David C Cook, 2011), 86.

No one will escape those flames of refinement or purification, according to Jesus, which is also what the Apostle Paul suggests in 1 Corinthians 3:14-15 when he says this:

> *"[Everyone's work] will be revealed with fire, and **the fire will test the quality of each person's work**. If what has been built survives, the builder will receive a reward. **If it is burned up, the builder will suffer loss but yet will be saved—even though only as one escaping through the flames**."*

This teaching is quite clear: Everyone will pass through the flames; both the righteous and the unrighteous. But what the fire burns up is not us but the works which have not been consistent with the character and nature of Christ within each of us.

We also find clues about the purpose and intention behind God's discipline and punishment in the book of Hebrews where we read in chapter 12, verses 7 through 11 the following:

> *"It is for discipline that you have to endure. **God is treating you as sons. For what son is there whom his father does not discipline?** If you are left without discipline—**and all undergo discipline**—then you are illegitimate children and not sons. Besides this, we have had earthly fathers who disciplined us and we respected them. Shall we not much more be subject to the Father of spirits and live? For they disciplined us for a short time as it seemed best to them, **but [God] disciplines us for our good, that we may share his holiness**. For the moment all discipline seems painful rather than pleasant, but later **it yields the peaceful fruit of righteousness to those who have been trained by it**." (emphasis mine)*

Let's take a moment to notice what is being said here. First, the author of Hebrews says that God disciplines those He loves, and that this discipline is an indication of our identity as the sons and daughters of God, adding that we "all undergo discipline", which affirms that all of us are, indeed, the Children of God. Next, he says that the reason God disciplines us is not for the sake of discipline itself, nor for the purpose of inflicting pain, nor to destroy us, but that God "disciplines us for our good, that we may share in [God's] holiness" and that this discipline leads to "the peaceful fruit of righteousness" for every single one of us.

So, whenever we read about anyone being cast into the flames of hell or the lake of fire, we must always keep in mind that this fire is intended to heal, restore, purify and redeem us, never to harm us, or torture us, or destroy us.

Simply put, God's intention, as we read in various scriptures, is to "make all things new" and to "restore all things unto Himself." Jesus is heralded as the "savior of the World" who intercedes on behalf of everyone—even those who murdered him—by praying, "Father, forgive them, for they know not what they do."

No one is more vocal and emphatic about God's plan to redeem and restore all of humanity than the Apostle Paul. In fact, his statements are some of the most unmistakably universalist in their tone than almost any others we find in the New Testament. Here are just a few examples:

> *"This is good and acceptable in the sight of our God our savior;* **Who will have all men to be saved, and to come to the knowledge of the truth.** *For there is one God, and one mediator between God and men, the man Christ Jesus:* **Who gave himself a ransom for all,** *to be testified in due time." (1 Tim. 2:3-6, KJV, emphasis mine)*

> *"This is a faithful saying and worthy of all acceptance. For to this end we both labor and suffer reproach, because* **we trust in the living God, Who is the Savior of all men, especially of those who believe.** *These things command and teach." (1 Tim. 4:9-11)*

"For as in Adam all died, even so in Christ all shall be made alive." (1 Cor. 15:22)

"Just as the result of one trespass was condemnation of all men, **so also the result of one act of righteousness was justification that brings life for all men.** *" (Rom. 5:18)*

"God was pleased to have all fullness dwell in Him, **and through Him to reconcile to Himself all things on earth or in heaven,** *by making peace through His blood, shed on the cross." (Col. 1:19-22)*

"For God was in Christ, **not counting our sins against us but reconciling the World to Himself.** *" (2 Cor. 5:19)*

We might also want to take a little more time with other passages from Paul's epistles which equally affirm the doctrine of Universal Reconciliation in ways that we might not notice at first. Those are found in Philippians 2:10-11 and in Romans chapter 11.

Let's start with what Paul says in Philippians:

"At the name of Jesus every knee should bow, of those in heaven, and those on earth, and of those under the earth, and that every tongue **should gladly confess** *that Jesus Christ is Lord to the glory of God the Father." (Phil. 2:10:11)*

Notice that I've emphasized the phrase "should gladly confess" in this passage because our English translations of this text have sadly left out the entirety of the Greek word *exomologeo*, which literally means "to acknowledge openly and joyfully" rather than merely to confess. So, the text suggests that a day is coming when everyone will—of their own free will—gladly and joyfully acknowledge that Jesus is Lord, which is especially significant when you realize that in his epistle to the Romans, this same Apostle

Paul affirms in chapter 10, verse 9 that "…if you confess with your mouth that Jesus is Lord…you will be saved."

The other emphatic passage where Paul exuberantly affirms the statement that all shall be saved is found in that same epistle to the Romans. But most of us miss this fact because we've been conditioned to read this letter a certain way. Specifically, we are not told that the letter was written using the rhetorical device of *prosopopoeia* in which the author communicates to their audience by speaking as another person having a conversation with someone who holds an opposing viewpoint. In other words, Romans is written as an imaginary debate between the Apostle Paul and another voice who, for all intents and purposes, is Saul the Pharisee.

Once we understand how this argumentation device is being used throughout the epistle of Romans, we start to notice how one voice declares a certain point of view which the next voice refutes and corrects. It's an ongoing dialog between the teacher of the Law and the Apostle of Christ regarding an important question: "Will all Israel be saved?" (see Romans 10)

As the two men debate back and forth, offering their perspectives and arguing their positions, the entire conversation culminates in Paul the Apostle concluding triumphantly that, yes, all Israel will be saved because God's plan is to save all people—both Jews and Gentiles—by extending saving mercy to everyone. Or, as Paul phrases it at the very end of Chapter 11 in verse 32:

> *"For God has committed them **all to disobedience, that He might have mercy on all.**"*

And how does Paul celebrate his victory over his opponent in this long debate? By doing a little dance in the end zone which immediately follows this verse above:

> *"Oh, the depth of the riches both of the wisdom and knowledge of God! How unsearchable are His judgments and His ways past finding out! For who has known the mind of the Lord? Or*

who has become His counselor? Or who has first given to Him,
and it shall be repaid to him? For of Him and through Him
and to Him are all things, to whom be glory forever! Amen."

But Paul is by no means the only Apostle to speak so strongly
of God's ultimate plan to redeem all mankind to Himself. We find
in the letter of 1 John such wondrous verses like:

*"[Jesus] is the propitiation for our sins, and **not for ours only***
but also for the whole world." (1 John 2:2)

And in the Gospel of John:

*"[Jesus] did not come to judge the world **but to save the***
world." (John 12:47)

And in the book of Hebrews:

*"**Jesus**, was made a little lower than the angels, for the suffer-*
*ing of death crowned with glory and honor, **that He, by the***
grace of God, might taste death for everyone." (Heb. 2:9)

And in the book of Acts:

*"[In Jesus Christ is] **the restoration of all things**, which God*
has spoken by the mouth of all His holy prophets since the
world began." (Acts 3:21)

As I mentioned earlier in this chapter, there are over 76 different verses in the Bible which loudly affirm the doctrine of Universal
Reconciliation, and we cannot explore each of them in as much detail as we might prefer in the limited space we have here.

However, by taking the time to share these verses that affirm
Universal Reconciliation I hope to make it clear that those who embrace this teaching do so not out of sentimentality nor by twisting

the scriptures to make them say what we want, nor by refusing to take the Bible seriously.

On the contrary, those of us who believe and teach the doctrine of Universal Reconciliation do so precisely because of what we read in the Old Testament scriptures, and what we hear from the mouth of Jesus, and what we see in the writings of the Apostle Paul, and John, and the book of Acts, and Hebrews, and yes, even the book of Revelation, about God's express desire and intention to redeem, restore and reconcile every single one of us to Himself, not matter how long it takes.

Because the gates of God's Kingdom are never shut, and to those outside the walls the Spirit cries out, "Come and drink, all who are thirsty, from the rivers of living water that flow from the throne of God!"[17]

Yes, God is that good. God is that loving. God is even more merciful and gracious than any of us could ever imagine.

---

17. See Revelations 21:22-27; 22: 1-5; 17.

CHAPTER 5

So As Through Fire:
Reconciliation through Purification

Sharon Baker Putt

Hell is a hot topic. In fact, around 58 % of Americans believe in hell as a place of eternal torment. So do about 82% of Evangelical Protestants.[1] Personally, I always took it for granted, never questioned its reality, its justice, or its duration. The thought of billions upon billions of people, the majority of all who have ever lived throughout history's millennia, burning forever and ever in hell, staggered my senses. How many of us have grown up hearing about and believing in the existence of hell, a fiery abyss that eternally burns without destroying, tortures without ceasing, punishes without respite, where the only thing that dies is the hope of release or reconciliation?[2]

Growing up a Baptist, I cannot count the number of times I sat in a pew watching a dark-suited preacher wipe sweat from

---

1. "Belief in Hell", Religious Landscape Study, Pew Research Center, accessed December 3, 2022, https://www.pewresearch.org/religion/religious-landscape-study/belief-in-hell/.

2. Sections of this essay are taken with permission from Sharon L. Baker, *Razing Hell: Rethinking Everything You've Been Taught About God's Wrath and Judgment* (Louisville: Westminster John Knox, 2010) and Sharon L. Baker Putt, *A Nonviolent Theology of Love: Peacefully Confessing the Apostles' Creed* (Minneapolis: Fortress, 2021).

his brow as he shouted out a good, old-fashioned fire and brimstone sermon. These types of messages have pervaded Christian
churches like insidious horror stories, laced with terrifying verbal
images that paint portraits of sinners standing before a terrible,
large, angry God with a long gray beard sitting upon a great, white
throne, pointing a judgmental finger in their direction. Trembling
with fear, they await the final pronouncement that ordains where
they will spend eternity—in the burning fires of eternal, conscious
torment, or in the idyllic paradise of heaven. We also have vivid
images of hell in our imaginations. We can picture the gates of hell,
fire, brimstone, and ghoulish looking bodies screaming in pain
while Satan (and sometimes God!) looks on with glee. Thanks to
Dante Alighieri's literary masterwork *The Divine Comedy*, this view
of hell gained great popularity throughout western Christendom
after the 14th century, yet it does not really have strong support
in Scripture. Jesus spoke of Gehenna in metaphorical, hyperbolic
terms.[3] The apostle Paul makes little mention of hell—a strange
lacuna if he considered it a central idea. And the early Christians
did not preach the gospel as salvation from hell; for them, salvation
meant life on earth in the divine kingdom.[4]

Surprisingly, the Christian tradition has no official view on
hell and views surrounding the topic differ widely throughout the
vast theological streams of Christian thought. Eternal Conscious
Torment theory (ECT), describes hell as a place of literal fire and
brimstone with its inhabitants suffering eternal, conscious torment.
Although preaching the torturous dangers of hell-fire seems to
serve as a great marketing strategy for evangelizing, it tries to moti-
vate faith through fear rather than through the invitation of a love
relationship with God. We must ask, however, whether God desires

---

3. For a discussion on the significance of Jesus's metaphorical use of Gehenna, a place
outside the walls of Jerusalem that Christians traditionally have translated as "hell,"
see Baker, *Razing Hell*, 128-130. For a great treatment of the history and meaning of
Gehenna and Jesus's use of the word, see Bradley Jersak, *Her Gates Will Never be Shut:
Hope, Hell, and the New Jerusalem* (Eugene, OR: Wipf & Stock, 2010).

4. Rita Nakashima Brock and Rebecca Ann Parker, *Saving Paradise: How Christianity
Traded Love for this World for Crucifixion and Empire* (Boston: Beacon, 2008), 13.

fear-based devotion or love-based devotion.[5] Jesus, the light of the world who exposes and overcomes the darkness, seems to teach the latter when he spoke the words, "Peace I leave with you; my peace I give to you. I do not give to you as the world gives. Do not let your hearts be troubled, and do not let them be afraid" (John 14:27). If not, then, the fear inducing terrors of final judgment and eternal damnation, how can we think about these last events that usher us into eternity?

The Eastern Orthodox Christian tradition imagines the final judgment as a time of purifying during which the final exposure of our darkness lies in the sanctifying light of divine fire, and in the purifying fire of judgment lies our hope for redemption. Although judgment will entail the pain of experiencing our lives and our sin exposed before God, the ultimate end of judgment is a process that leads to ultimate redemption rather than a condemnatory verdict. We stand before God as both the sheep and goat described in Jesus's parable in the Gospels, while the all-consuming fire of God burns away the impurities (the "goat") that infect our lives. The fire burns up the goat and leaves behind the purified sheep in all of us. As righteous, new creations, imbued with a new innocence, we will see the goodness and love of God and freely consent to enter into the divine kingdom. The love of God will turn us all toward God so that, as Augustine says, we will find our true rest in God.[6] This purgation process of standing in the divine fire will prepare us for eternal life with God, therefore, fulfilling the scriptural promise that we will experience "what no eye has seen, nor ear heard, nor the human heart conceived, what God has prepared for those who love him" (1 Cor. 2:9). This view stresses the significance of fire and its purifying qualities.

Indeed, fire and God are intimately connected in the Bible. For instance, God is a consuming or devouring fire (Deut. 4:24; Ezek.

---

5. Thomas Jay Oord, *God Can't: How to Believe in God and Love after Tragedy, Abuse, and Other Evils* (Grasmere, ID: SacraSage, 2019), 151.

6. Augustine, *Confessions,* I.1.1; John Polkinghorne, *The God of Hope and the End of the World* (New Haven: Yale University Press, 2003), 130-34.

1:27; 8:2; Heb. 12:29). Fire flows out from God's presence (Dan. 7:10). God appears as fire in a burning bush to Moses (Exod. 3:2-3). A pillar of fire symbolizes God's presence (Exod. 12:21-22). God's tongue, breath, eyes, and mouth are like flames of fire (Isa. 30:27, 33; Rev. 2:18). Flames of fire issue from God's nostrils and voice (Deut. 4:36; Isa. 65:5; Jer. 23:29). God's glory is a flame of fire (Zech. 2:5). Ezekiel sees God as a flashing fire that burns with splendor like glowing amber (Ezek. 1:4, 13-14). Both Daniel and John envision God sitting on a throne of fire, with a face shining like lightning, with eyes like flaming torches (Dan. 7:9-11; Rev. 1:14-15; 4:5). For Malachi, God is the fire that purifies and refines (Mal. 4:1). [7] That said, the fire of God, whether it issues from God or surrounds and envelops God, serves a very significant purpose in general.

Upon further investigation of scripture, we see that the fire of God burns and devours wickedness like stubble, completely annihilating it (Isa. 1:25-27). Fire also cleanses and purifies what remains (Isa. 6:6-7; Dan. 3:20-27). When Isaiah came before the throne of God, the seraphim (which, by the way, is the plural form of the Hebrew word for fire) that continually surround God touched his lips with a live burning coal so that his sin was blotted out and he was made clean, ready to serve God in ministry. Zechariah prophesies that God will put the wicked "into the fire and refine them as one refines silver, and test them as gold is tested" (Zech. 13:9). The apostle Peter supports this purifying process in the New Testament when he writes about the testing of our faith through fire (1 Pet. 1:7).

We also see that the fire of God will not burn up whatever is righteous and pure. For instance, Isaiah reminds us in beautiful prose that "When you (righteous people of God) pass through the waters, I will be with you; and through the rivers, they shall not overwhelm you; when you walk through the fire you shall

---

7. The fire of God as described in these verses corrects, heals, cleanses, and purifies. See also Jersak, *Her Gates Will Never be Shut*, 75.

not be burned, and the flame shall not consume you" (Isa. 43:2). Remember that Daniel's friends walked about in a fire that devoured the men who threw them in, but they themselves were unscathed. Why? Because they were righteous before God and the fire only burns evil, wickedness, and unrighteousness. Consequently, they were safe from its destruction—there was nothing impure to burn up (Dan. 3:20-27).

In a nutshell, we see so far that fire not only surrounds God, but God *is* a consuming fire.[8] The fire of God burns up evil and wickedness so that it no longer exists. What remains, if anything, is pure and righteous. Fire does not consume, devour, or even scorch the pure and the righteous. But what does this divine fire have to do with hell? Many Christians who object to the retributive, violent, angry image of God that views of ECT promote, believe instead that hell entails the fire of God consuming the wickedness and evil that permeate our souls, leaving us righteous and pure, ready for eternity with God through Christ.[9]

Theories of hell as a purifying fire in the presence of God rather than as an eternal place of evil, fire, and brimstone go back to the earliest Christian traditions. Early Christian theologians such as Origen, Isaac of Nineveh, and Gregory of Nyssa articulate hell as a purification in the presence of God, the all-consuming fire. The divine fire, specifically in relation to hell and salvation, serves several purposes, all for the benefit of God's creation.

First, rather than a fire of wrath, the fire manifests God's love and mercy. St. Isaac of Nineveh tells us that "just because the terms 'wrath', 'anger', and 'hatred', and the rest are used of the Creator in the Bible, we should not imagine that He actually does anything in anger, hatred, or zeal. Many figurative terms are used of God in

---

8. See also Gregory of Nyssa, "On the Resurrection, and the Judgment, the Fire of Hell, and Punishments," in *The Complete Ante-Nicene & Nicene and Post-Nicene Church Fathers Collection*, ed. Philip Schaff (Catholic Way Publishing, 2014). Hereafter cited as *ANPNF*.

9. Jesus said that "everyone will be salted with fire" (Mark 9:49). Those who know Christ should welcome the fire as the passionate love of God to purify and those who do not know Christ will learn of this love as their wickedness is burned away. See Jersak, 63.

the Scriptures, terms which are far removed from His true nature." Instead, "among all God's actions there is none which is not entirely a matter of mercy, love, and compassion: this constitutes the beginning and end of His dealings with us."[10] St. Isaac teaches that the efficacy and power of God's mercy and passionate love extend even to the demons in ways that are only advantageous and merciful to us and that are "directed towards the single eternal good."[11] No amount of evil exists that can overcome the extent and extravagance of the burning flame of God's mercy, goodness, and love. In fact, if evil can overcome the power of God to save, we might need to question God's omnipotence in fulfilling the divine plan of redemption.[12]

Second, the divine fire acts as a pedagogical tool to educate and correct those who walk through the flames. Again, we turn to Isaac of Nineveh who argued that the fire of God acts in a fatherly way, with passionate love that makes us aware of our sinfulness, teaches us the gravity of sin, transforms us, and draws us to God.[13] For Gregory of Nyssa, the divine fire exposes the darkness of sin and burns away the passionate and irrational aspects of our nature. He believes we see the history of all our foul deeds, and convicted in our conscience, corrected in our attitude, we act as our own accuser (Rom. 2:15). This pedagogical process that makes us aware of the impact and evil of our sin in the face of the compassionate love of God, will result in the recognition of Jesus Christ as the redeemer of sin and as the author and benefactor of eternal life.[14]

---

10. St. Isaac of Nineveh, 'The Second Part,' chapters IV-XLI, *Corpus Scriptorum Christianorum* Orientalium, vol. 55, trans. Sebastian Brock (Lovanii: In Aedibus Peeters, 1995), XXXIX.19 and 22.

11. Ibid, XXXIX.3.

12. Jersak, 111 and 148.

13. Ibid, XXXIX.8 and 14.

14. Gregory of Nyssa, "On the Resurrection, and the Judgment," chapter X.4. Opinion between theologians differs about the duration of these processes. Gregory and St. Isaac, for example, believe that the process of standing in the divine fire will be temporary and the duration depends upon the amount of purification needed.

Third, the divine fire heals. Gregory of Nyssa describes the fire of God as a painful means to a good end, comparing it to a surgeon's knife, which causes pain, yet heals the ailment. Just as the knife cuts away a tumor and heals the patient, so the divine fire burns away evil, delivering every person from vice with the healing flames of God's love. He writes that when evil has been purged and utterly removed from us "by the healing processes worked out by the fire, then every one of the things which make up our conception of the good will come to take their place; incorruption, that is, and life, and honor, and grace, and glory, and everything else that we conjecture is to be seen in God, and in His image."[15] Even though the experience of fire and confrontation with personal sin may inflict the pain of awareness and remorse, the burning passion of God's love heals that pain with mercy and grace that cleanses and purifies.

Fourth, the divine fire cleanses and purifies those who stand in its presence. Gregory of Nyssa claims that the fire of God burns away all wickedness, bringing us back to our primal state, what he calls "that universal form which God stamped upon us at the beginning"…"when it never received evil."[16] He compares this process to refining gold, during which the goldsmith heats the impure gold in a crucible over the fire until all the impurities rise to the surface. He scrapes off the impurities, remelts the gold in the refiner's fire, scrapes off the impurities again, and continues the process until finally, he can see his face reflected in the pure gold. Just as the gold is purified for the good of a product, so God refines us in

---

15. Gregory of Nyssa, *On the Soul and the Resurrection* (Minneapolis: Aeterna, 2016), 63. See also Morwena Ludlow, *Universal Salvation: Eschatology in the Thought of Gregory of Nyssa and Karl Rahner* (Oxford: Oxford University Press, 2000), 84-5, 107, 109. For Clement of Alexandria, the fire of God is corrective rather than punitive. See *Stromata* VI.6, 14; VII.16, 102; VI. 6, 46 in *ANPNF;* Hans Urs Von Balthasar, *Dare We Hope 'That All Men Be Saved?',* trans. Dr. David Kipp ad Rev. Lothar Krauth (San Francisco: Ignatius, 1988), 62-3. Origen contends that all will pass through the flame (per Paul and Christ), but that those flames will be curative and complete for all eternity (Origen, *Contra Celsius,* VI.11-13; V.15-16 for example in *ANPNF.*)

16. Gregory of Nyssa, *On the Soul and the Resurrection,* 62; Morwenna Ludlow, *Universal Salvation,* 86. She quotes Gregory's commentary on 1 Cor. 15:28.

the divine fire "only to get the good separated from the evil and to attract it into the communion of blessedness."[17]

Applying the Hebrew scriptures to the entire human race, Gregory also uses the metaphor of cleansing in the divine fire. God calls all people to this divine cleansing in Isaiah 1:18, which urges us to "come now, let us reason together, says the Lord, though your sins are as scarlet, they will be as white as snow; though they are red like crimson, they will be like wool."[18] In a conversation with Gregory, his sister, Macrina, points out that some of us, through wisdom, are cleansed from evil in this life, and others, after this life, are cleansed by the fire so that God can offer to all people the eternal blessings of life in Christ.[19] This cleansing and purifying, although potentially painful like a surgeon's knife, occurs for our good, for God's glory, and for the transformation of all creation by annihilating evil—which brings us to the next purpose for divine fire.

Fifth, the divine fire annihilates evil, leaving renewal and transformation in its wake. The traditional annihilation theory of hell, at least one rendering of it, makes the claim that hell, Hades, all demons, the devil himself, and all unsaved people will suffer annihilation in the Lake of Fire after the judgment. With the purification theory, however, I make the claim that annihilation does take place, but the Lake of Fire serves as a metaphor for the total annihilation of evil and only evil—not the persons whom it has infected. The fire of God, in passion and love, seeking only the renewing transformation of all things completely destroys and annihilates evil so that it no longer exists, yet, at the same time, purifies and preserves all humanity, transforming it through fire into its original, pre-sin condition.[20] Cardinal Ratzinger describes this transfor-

---

17. Ibid., 37-8. See also Gregory of Nyssa, "On the Resurrection, and the Judgment," chapter XIII; Isa. 4:4; Mal. 3:3.

18. I like this verse in the NASB version.

19. Gregory of Nyssa, On the Soul and the Resurrection, 59.

20. Joseph Ratzinger, Eschatology: Death and Eternal Life, trans. Michael Waldstein, 2nd ed. (Washington, DC: The Catholic University of America Press, 1988), 224-27, 229.

mation through fire, stating that the judging fire of God transforms us and conforms us to his own glorified body; "through the transforming power of the Lord himself, whose burning flame cuts free our closed-off heart, melting it, and pouring it into a new mold" we are "made fit for the living organism of his body."[21] When all is accomplished, evil will no longer exist and all creation will live in the transformed newness of life with God in Christ for all eternity. This vision of final purification or judgment as "hell" and the reconciliation and restoration of all created things brings glory to God in Christ for "every knee will bow and every tongue will confess that Jesus is Lord to the glory of God the father" (Phil. 2:10-11).[22]

I Corinthians 3:10-15 provides us with scriptural support for this fiery educational, healing, and purifying process. This passage reveals that every person builds upon the foundation of Jesus Christ. The passage continues: "Now if any person builds upon the foundation with gold, silver, precious stones, wood, hay, straw, each person's work will show it, because it is to be revealed with fire; and the fire itself will test the quality of each person's work. If anyone's work which he has built upon it remains, he shall receive a reward. If any person's work is burned up, he shall suffer loss; but *he himself shall be saved, yet so as through fire*" (italics added). It seems that in the final judgment, *everyone* will go through the fire—through the fire that surrounds God, comes from God, and *is* God. Because fire burns away impurities, any pure works built upon the foundation will remain and the person will receive a reward. The impure works do not survive the fire. The person himself, however, will still be saved, yet only after going through the flames. If God is the devouring fire, then standing in the presence

---

Gregory of Nyssa, "On the Resurrection, and the Judgment," chapter XIII and Gregory of Nyssa, *On the Soul and the Resurrection*, 37.

21. Ratzinger, *Eschatology*, 229.

22. For a more complete treatment of this view, read Sharon L. Baker, *Razing Hell: Rethinking Everything You've Been Taught about Salvation and the Cross* (Louisville: Westminster John Knox, 2010). See also scriptures claiming universal salvation for all creation: 1 Tim. 4:9-10; 1 John 2:1-2; Rom. 8:20-21.

of God is to stand in the fire. Every person will eventually stand before God, with or without Jesus, to give an account of his or her life (1 Cor. 4:5; 2 Cor. 5:10-11). To stand in God's presence entails standing in the flames. To stand in the flames means burning away chaff, wickedness, and sinfulness.[23]

In order to give you a clearer picture of what the biblical account of standing in the consuming fire of God's presence at the judgment might look like, I'll give you a hypothetical and metaphorical story based upon what we have discussed in this chapter. Picture a person who has committed much evil in his life, someone who rejected Jesus while living, someone who may have abused a spouse or child, a person who perhaps committed terrible acts of terrorism against innocent people. Imagine a person, any person, who you would like to see get what's coming to him (or her)—and it's judgment day. For the sake of the illustration, let's call this person, Otto Luck—an international leader who, under the cover of his religion, has pre-empted wars and terrorized nations with his arrogant dominance, leading to the death of thousands upon thousands of men, women, and children. He prepares to go into the presence of God. His attitude smacks of rebellion, anger, and hatred because he knows the time for payback has arrived. He knows that God is going to judge harshly and throw him in eternal torture as punishment and he hates God for it.

Otto dies and enters into the throne room of God; glaring flames of fire confront him, so bright and hot he cannot see anything other than bright light. His anger and rebellion turn to sheer terror. He moves closer to the flames and as he does so, he realizes that the blazing fire *is* God. The closer he gets to God, the more deeply he feels, not God's hatred or judgment, but God's love—a love of such magnitude that, with its abundance, seems at first like wrath, judging him for his deficiency, and with its purity, serves

---

23. For more on how the purification process functions for Christians who have already reconciled to God through Christ, see Sharon L. Baker, *Executing God: Rethinking Everything You've Been Taught about Salvation and the Cross* (Louisville: Westminster John Knox, 2016).

as a hell, punishing him for his depravity. But as his sin is burned away by the fire, he realizes it's not wrath and punishment at all, but instead is God's love and mercy, both acting as judgment, so extravagant, so abundant, so incomprehensible that it completely overwhelms Otto. Then he hears a voice from the fire. The voice does *not* say, "You evil, vile murderer! I am going to get you now. Revenge, punishment, and torture forever and ever!" Instead, he hears God say with sorrow forged from love, "I have loved you with an everlasting love. But look at your life; what have you done?"

Totally undone by God's unorthodox approach, Otto falls to his face, still afraid but with his hatred replaced by remorse. As his life flashes before his eyes, he sees all the victims, mothers crying for lost sons, children begging for the return of their murdered fathers, the eighteen-year-old boy dying alone, mortally wounded, wanting his mother. Otto hears their screams, sees their bloody, battered bodies, and listens as they cry out for mercy. And he knows he gave none. Yet, here he stands in the fire of God, receiving what he never gave. He looks to his right and sees his victims. Still in the fire, God makes him go to each one and lay his hand upon their hearts. As he does so, he feels all of their pain, all of their disappointments, all of their fear, and knows that he has caused it all. Within the crowd of victims, the last one he has left to touch, he sees Jesus.

When he places his hand on Jesus' heart, he not only feels the pain, sorrow, and the disappointment he has caused him, but he feels the unconditional love that Jesus has for him, Otto. All the while the fire of God burns, devouring Otto's wickedness and evil deeds. Lest you think he gets off too easy, this is hell for him. With gnashing teeth, and uncontrollable weeping, his heart breaks, and he cries out in utter remorse, in unmitigated repentance, inconsolably grief stricken, knowing he can never undo the damage he has caused. Seeing his repentance and the unendurable and seemingly unending pain he feels as the fire burns off the chaff of his evil deeds, the victims are vindicated. The one thing victims most often wish for is that their offender feels remorse and knows the terrible pain he has caused them. Otto's immense remorse and pain at the knowledge of his sin against them, satisfies this need. George MacDonald, one of my favorite theologians, explains the pain of the fire, which I call "hell," saying that "the fire of God, which is His essential being, His love, His creative power, is a fire unlikely in its earthly symbol in this, that it is only at a distance it burns—that the further from Him, it burns the worse." The farther a person stands from God in that day the more pain the fire causes as it burns away the impurities. Otto doesn't get away with murder; he doesn't get to take a walk without suffering any consequences. He burns in God's eternal fire. The more he burns the closer he stands to God until finally, he stands close to God, purified, free from sin, and ready to hear God's next words.

Then Otto hears God say, "I have forgiven you. Will you be reconciled to me and to those you have wronged?" Barely able to answer, Otto nods his head in utter disbelief. Much to his astonishment, God asks his victims to draw near to him and to put their hands on his heart. As they touch him, each one feels Otto's pain, his fears, his disappointments; they can hear his cries as a child, know his shame as an adult, and they understand who he was as an evil ruler. Themselves forgiven and embraced by the love of God, they extend that same kind of grace to Otto, forgiving him his sins against them. At last, Jesus stands before him, touches Otto's heart and says, "I have loved you with an everlasting love. Will you enter into my kingdom and be restored to God." And Otto, fully righteous and free from sin and its effects, of course accepts (wouldn't any righteous person no longer enslaved to sin choose Christ?). He has been judged by the fire of love; he has walked through the fire of God's "wrath"; he has been purified by the fire of God's mercy. He freely chooses to receive the forgiveness, reconciliation, and restoration given to all who walk through the flames, and he enters the kingdom of God, tested by fire, forgiven by grace. And, God has changed his name from Otto Luck to something new, renewed, and transformed (Rev. 2:17; 3:12). For Otto and for all people, God's judgment takes the form of inexplicable, extravagant love that brings a person to repentance and into an eternal relationship with the relational God—a God who keeps redemption open for all creation

The purification view from this perspective respects human freedom, yet at the same time, sees God's will to save all people fulfilled (1 Tim. 2:4; 2 Pet. 3:9). We could actually say with the writer of Philippians that every knee will choose to bow and every tongue will choose to confess that Jesus Christ is Lord. With this alternative view of hell, we maximize the powerful effectiveness of the cross and the power of God to save. Jesus wins the final and absolute victory over evil and death. He breaks the power of sin. He fully, completely, absolutely accomplishes God's mission to reconcile the world to himself. Glory to God—truly!

CHAPTER 6

Constructing a Biblical Theology of Hell:
The Case for Conditional Immortality

Chad Bahl

God has been made so cruel, and this doctrine is so unthinkable that it has probably created more atheists and caused more weak believers to fall away than any other false teaching. The dread of hell has caused misery and mental anguish to countless millions and instead of the horror of hell turning many to God... many millions have been turned away.
—William West, "The Resurrection and Immortality"

How can Christians possibly portray a deity of such cruelty and vindictiveness whose ways include inflicting everlasting torture upon His creatures, however sinful they may have been?
—Clark Pinnock, "The Destruction
of the Finally Impenitent"

What is at Stake

Abrasive words are not spared by those who disagree with the traditional doctrine of eternal conscious torment. Though I side with the above criticisms, I have refrained from quoting even harsher verbiage. Certainly, the debate over the doctrine of hell evokes passion from all sides. But why is this? What exactly is at stake as theologians spar over what, on its face, seems like just one more topic regarding which the Bible does not provide definitive clarity?

Speaking as one who affirms the doctrine of conditional immortality[1], I see much at stake. First and foremost, the belief that our Heavenly Father would sentence any man to an eternity of conscious pain and anguish *for any reason* calls into question the very character of God. Few Christians would disagree that the God of the Bible is one of love.[2] But how can it be loving to send a temporal being to an eternal torture chamber? As ones created Imago Dei, and endowed with the prevenient grace of the Holy Spirit, we all have a sense of right and wrong. We have an inkling of morality and of what it means to love (though perhaps dimly as in the reflection of a mirror).[3] We look at the great atrocities of history and see them as counter to even the most obtuse definitions. No degree of love can be found in the gas chambers, torturous experimentation, and myriad other inhumanities of the holocaust. We see no love in the use of painful and disfiguring chemical weapons by Russia in Syria and most recently in Ukraine. We even look at the torment of animals as so revolting that only the lowliest of humans can perform such acts. Clearly, the concepts of torture and love are antithetical.

But somehow the traditionalist is able to marry these two within the character of the Divine. She might argue that God is equally just as He is loving, and this may allow her to reason for the legitimacy of the eternal suffering view of hell. But while receiving

---

1. Simply defined, conditional immortality entails the belief that those who die without faith in Christ will not exist eternally. There are several flavors of this view that have been espoused over time. Key differences among them deal with whether God is active in "annihilating" the unrepentant or if He passively stops sustaining their existence. Most Conditionalists (as well as most Universalists) also acknowledge the biblical texts that affirm suffering after judgement. Though the length of time is debated, all would agree that there is a just end.

2. 1 John 4:16 Today's New International Version

3. 1 Corinthians 13:12 (TNIV).

justice for our sins might very well result in separation from God,[4] this essay aims to demonstrate that nowhere in the Bible does it necessitate unending conscious suffering.

On the Immortality of the Soul

If conditional immortality is to be argued, what must first be addressed is the question of how so many scholars of the Church could have possibly gotten it wrong. The answer arguably lies in the teachings of Hellenism, which were contemporary to the formation of Christian thought. As addressed previously in this volume, the major influence here is the thinking that the soul is naturally immortal. Plato clearly taught so. In fact, he is a primary source cited when philosophers argue the indestructibility of the soul. In his dialogue *Phaedo,* Plato presents his teacher, Socrates, encouraging the reader that there is nothing to fear in death and that the soul eternally continues on. He provides four separate arguments in support of this view.[5]

Augustine, following the philosophic heritage of Plato, also formed an argument from intellectualism for the immortality of the soul in his writing *The City of God.*[6] This was a belief John Calvin would also adopt.[7] With the opinion that the soul is by nature immortal comes the necessary conclusion that it can never be destroyed. In other words, if one dies and is not destined to spend eternity with God in Heaven, there must be a place for that soul to reside.

But is the doctrine of the soul's immortality supported in Scripture? An honest review of popular passages may compel us to conclude in the negative.

---

4. Matthew 7:21-23 (TNIV).

5. Plato, *Phaedo,* 69e-84b. See the Argument from Opposites, the Theory of Recollection, the Argument from Affinity, and the Argument Based on Forms.

6. Augustine, *The City of God*, trans. Marcus Dods (Edinburgh: T. & T. Clark, 1871), vol. 2 ch. 23.

7. John Calvin, *Psychopannychia* (1534).

Scripture and the Natural Mortality of the Soul

Beginning in the book of Genesis, we see conditional immortality taught. Among the punishments Adam and Eve received for their transgressions against God was the removal of the guarantee of an everlasting existence. *"And the LORD God said, 'The man has now become like one of us, knowing good and evil. He must not be allowed to reach out his hand and take also from the tree of life and eat, and live forever.*[8]*'"* Immortality was a gift and, at least in their current state of sin, the option of achieving it was withdrawn from our most ancient ancestors.

In fact, the threat of ultimate destruction permeates the Scriptures. Just a handful of verses giving reference to this are cited below:

> *****Matthew 10:28** - *Do not be afraid of those who kill the body but cannot kill the soul. Rather, be afraid of the One who can destroy both soul and body in hell.*

> *****James 4:12** - *There is only one Lawgiver and Judge, the one who is able to save and destroy.*

> ***2 Thessalonians 1:8-9** - *He will punish those who do not know God and do not obey the gospel of our Lord Jesus. They will be punished with everlasting destruction and shut out from the presence of the Lord and from the glory of his might...*

> ***Philippians 3:18-19a** - *For, as I have often told you before and now tell you again even with tears, many live as enemies of the cross of Christ. Their destiny is destruction...*[9]

---

8. Genesis 3:22 (TNIV).

9. See also John 3:16, Romans 6:23, 2 Timothy 1:10.

As alluded to above, it is not just the New Testament that speaks to the mortality of the soul. The Old Testament is rife with the same language:

> ***Genesis 3:19** - *By the sweat of your brow you will eat your food until you return to the ground, since from it you were taken; for dust you are and to dust you will return.*

> ***Psalms 1:5-6** - *Therefore the wicked will not stand in the judgement, nor sinners in the assembly of the righteous. For the Lord watches over the way of the righteous, but the way of the wicked leads to destruction.*

> ***Malachi 4:1** - *"Surely the day is coming; it will burn like a furnace. All the arrogant and every evildoer will be stubble, and the day that is coming will set them on fire," says the Lord Almighty. "Not a root or branch will be left of them."*

Taken on its face, the Bible seems to be warning the sinner that the organic consequence of his transgressions is destruction[10], not torment. It is hard to imagine another natural reading of the above passages. Plato added much to philosophic discourse, but the authors of Scripture would seem to take issue with his view of the afterlife.

On the contrary to traditional thinking, the Bible offers immortality to only those who uphold the Good News. Paul opines in his letter to Timothy, *"This grace was given us in Christ Jesus before the beginning of time, but it has now been revealed through the appearing of our Savior, Christ Jesus, who has destroyed death and*

---

10. Given the nature of any eschatological assertion, it is best to approach any interpretation with care and modesty. The need to interpret passages such as Matthew 28:10 as referencing "irreversible destruction" is laid out well in multiple articles written on the topic. See Clark Pinnock in his contribution to *Four Views on Hell* (Grand Rapids, MI: Zondervan, 1996).

has brought life and immortality to light through the gospel."[11] If the Gospel holds the key to immortality, it is logical to assume the rejection of that same Gospel brings the punishment of death.

The doctrine of conditional immortality is given further support through how Jesus described hell in the Gospels. When He referred to the punishment of the sinner, He used the word Gehenna, which has since been directly translated as "hell." Gehenna has widely been viewed as having been a garbage dump outside the city of Jerusalem: at the dump, the fire constantly burned, but whatever was thrown into it was immediately incinerated. It has also been accepted (perhaps more accurately) as a place of pagan human sacrifice.[12] So, in Matthew's Gospel, when Jesus says the body and soul of the unbeliever would be destroyed in "Gehenna" (or "hell"), His listeners would immediately relate the referenced punishment to the process of consumption by fire. Jesus refers to Gehenna a total of eleven times throughout the gospels. In all but one instance (where he is calling the Pharisees children of hell[13]), Jesus is illustrating the judgment that awaits those who reject the way of life.

Problem Passages

So, if the teachings of Jesus regarding hell imply conditional immortality and if several other passages appear to support that view, where do opponents of the doctrine find their biblical support? Let us look at a couple of passages traditionalists use.

> ***Isaiah 66:24** - And they will go out and look on the dead bodies of those who rebelled against me; the worms that eat them will not die, the fire that burns them will not be quenched, and they will be loathsome to all mankind.*

---

11. 2 Timothy 1:9b-10 (TNIV).

12. For a thorough discussion on this matter, please reference the proceeding chapter by Chris Loewen.

13. Matthew 23:15 (TNIV).

Advocates of the eternal torment view point out the worm that inflicts the suffering "will not die." Further, "the fire... will not be quenched." Does this not indicate eternal hellfire? Maybe. It says nothing about eternal consciousness for the non-believer. Look back at Jesus' Gehenna reference. The fires "never went out," but clearly what was burned was destroyed. What is more, the writer of Isaiah provides his own clarity. The first part of the verse states, "And they will go out and look on the dead bodies of those who rebelled against me." Rather than a verse that supports the traditional view of hell, Isaiah 66:24 speaks against it. If the bodies of the condemned are dead, how could they possibly be suffering?

Revelation 14:11 - *And the smoke of their torment will rise for ever and ever. There will be no rest day or night for those who worship the beast and its image, or for anyone who receives the mark of its name.*

On its face, this passage may seem slightly more troubling for the conditionalist. A closer look will ease the mind, as the only endless event described here is the ascending "smoke of [the] torment" of the lost soul. Surely its presence will be a sign to the believer of the righteous judgment of God, but this in no way indicates the objects of His punishment will be writhing in pain underneath. That there will be no rest for those who receive the mark of the beast cannot be a reflection of the eternal state as what need is there for day or night in eternity (Rev. 22:5)?

Revelation 20:10 - *And they marched up over the broad plain of the earth and surrounded the camp of the saints and the beloved city, but fire came down from heaven and consumed them, and the devil who had deceived them was thrown into the lake of fire and sulfur where the beast and the false prophet were, and they will be tormented day and night forever and ever.*

This passage, again, appears to speak to eternal conscious suffering. Even if that would be the case, it must be noted that the only ones receiving such an extreme punishment make up the unholy trinity. In the case of the beast and the false prophet, Fudge points out to us that, "they are not actual people but representations of persecuting civil government and of corrupting false religion."[14] He goes on to state that since, "the language here is symbolic...a literal interpretation is impossible."[15]

> **Luke 16:19-31** - *There was a rich man who was dressed in purple and fine linen and lived in luxury every day. At his gate was laid a beggar named Lazarus... The time came when the beggar died and the angels carried him to Abraham's side. The rich man also died and was buried. In Hades, where he was in torment, he looked up and saw Abraham far away, with Lazarus by his side. So he called to him, "Father Abraham, have pity on me..." But Abraham replied, "Son, remember that in your lifetime you received your good things, while Lazarus received bad things, but now he is comforted here and you are in agony..." He answered, "Then I beg you, father, send Lazarus to my family, for I have five brothers. Let him warn them, so that they will not also come to this place of torment."*

The story of the *Rich Man and Lazarus* is frequently cited as a defense against conditional immortality. If the rich man is suffering in hell, then this parable provides proof positive of the eternal state of the unbeliever. The passage, however, cannot be about final punishment. This is made clear for two reasons. The rich man is in Hades, not hell. That Hades is an intermediary place between death and judgement is made clear in Revelation 20:13, which describes how, "*death and Hades gave up the dead that were in them,*

---

14. Edward Fudge, "The Fire That Consumes," (Fallbrook, CA: Verdict Publications, 1982), 303.
15. Ibid., 304.

and everyone was judged according to what they had done." Secondly, the rich man's brothers are still alive. This is another indication that the Final Judgement had not yet occurred. If the rich man was suffering eternally in hell, then he somehow got there long before he was supposed to.

Taken at face value, once the veil of traditionalism and cultural influences has been pulled away, there remains little support in Scripture for the doctrine of eternal conscious torment.

A Growing Dissent

As referenced in this book's preface as well as by Robert Cornwall in Chapter 1, we see evidence of three major views evolving out of early Church history regarding the destiny of the non-believer: hell as eternal suffering, conditional immortality and universal restoration. It is clear the former-most has become the majority view of theologians over time. However, there remains a thread of vocal dissent over the centuries that affirm conditional immortality, and those voices are worth listening to.

*70-100 A.D. - "…the creation of men will enter into the fire of testing, and many will fall away and perish." **(Didache 16:5)**

*70-132 A.D. - "For it is a road of eternal death with punishment, and in it are things that destroy men's souls." **(Epistle of Barnabas 20:1)**

*95-140 A.D. - "Fear him who, after killing you, has the power to throw soul and body into Gehenna of fire." **(2 Clement 5:4)**

*100-165 A.D. - "For those things which exist after God… have the nature of decay and are such as may be blotted out and cease to exist." **Justin Martyr**

*1608-1674 A.D. - "What could be more just than that he who sinned in his whole person, should die in his whole person…it is evident that the saint and believers of old, the patriarchs, prophets and apostles, without exception, held this doctrine." **John Milton**

*1695 A.D. - "By death, some men understand endless torments in hellfire, but it seems a strange way understanding a law which requires the plainest and directest of words, that by death should be meant eternal life in misery." **John Locke**

*1988 A.D. - "The ultimate annihilation of the wicked should at least be accepted as a legitimate, biblically founded alternative to…eternal conscious torment." **John Stott**

In more recent times, conditional immortality has been an integral part the doctrine of the Advent Christian Church, the Church of God, the Seventh-day Adventist Church and the Jehovah's Witnesses.[16]

Edward Fudge, in his extensive work, *The Fire that Consumes*, acknowledges the doctrine of eternal suffering as the majority view but opines:

Today we see the tide turning the other direction. With the growing belief that Western culture (including the church) has assimilated a dualistic view of man from pagan speculations of Greek philosophy, alongside a rising conviction that the Bible presents quite a different view…the doctrine of final punishment is also coming under more and more to the forefront…the result is a growing dissatisfaction with the traditionalist doctrine of everlasting conscious torment;

---

16. Ibid., 397-98.

at the same time there is a resurgence of biblical study and renewed exegetical zeal.[17]

We must be willing to be the oar to right a misdirected boat when presented with sufficient evidence. We should feel compelled to take a stand when dogmas bely sound doctrine. And this call to action is not just for the pastors in the pulpit or the academics in ivory towers. It is for you and me. The one who chooses not to study these matters on some level makes a real decision (consciously or not) to surrender their access to knowledge of the divine to those who are willing to do the work for them. Put more simply, if you choose not to study doctrine, someone will do it for you… and tell you what to believe. Nearly every Christian has an idea of how God "works" and who God is, but very few can explain why they believe what they do, as is our calling.[18] They are not able to separate out what they have been taught during Sunday school from what the Bible says. And this is exactly how bad doctrine becomes generational. It is precisely how a believer who knows for a fact that the God of the Bible is loving and good may at the same time be convinced the He would allow someone to be tormented for eternity for refusing to believe in Him. Those who choose not to constructively analyze their belief systems do themselves a disservice and, more detrimentally, risk failing to accurately portray a God of love to a world in need.

A Small Distinction with Large Implications

As I begin to wrap up my essay, I want to briefly return to the topic alluded to in a footnote above. It is the minor detail of nomenclature. I have been intentional in this essay to refer to the view for which I am advocating as "conditional immortality." Others refer to this same perspective as "annihilationism." I must express

---

17. Ibid., 408
18. 1 Peter 3:15 (TNIV).

my personal disconcertment with this terminology. Hopefully the reader will find my reasons justifiable.

"Conditional immortality" references the current state of un-redeemed mankind. It is passive and simply descriptive. "Annihila-tion," on the other hand, connotes the act of inflicting punishment. Some may observe, since Conditionalists believe those who do not receive salvation will ultimately perish, this is a distinction with-out a difference. I think however, in the search for a compelling view of the destination for the impenitent, there are significant implications.

God always wants to preserve life and not destroy it. Indeed, it is He who do does not desire "anyone to perish, but everyone to come to repentance."[19] God searches out the lost and weeps when separation occurs.[20] God desires no retribution and benefits none by punishment inflicted. A primary argument against condition-alism, particularly from those who would define their theology as Open and Relational, is that the act of annihilation is inconsistent with a God who is defined by His love. From my vantage point, it is much different for God, who is "sustaining all things by his pow-erful word,"[21] to not grant immortality as a reward for faith then it is for Him to actively incinerate those who reject such belief. As John Stackhouse rightly puts it, "People thus don't suffer and die in hell because God chooses to torture and kill them. Suffering and death are the sheer consequences in this moral universe for our sins."[22]

A Look at Universal Restoration

As referenced above, a second alternative to the doctrine of eternal suffering (which also has substantial historical support) is that of

---

19. 2 Peter 3:9 (TNIV).

20. See Luke 15:3-7, Luke 19: 41-44

21. Heb. 1:3 (TNIV).

22. John G. Stackhouse, Jr., "Is Hell Eternal?," *Think Better* (blog), March 17, 2021, https://www.johnstackhouse.com/post/is-hell-eternal.

Universal Restoration. In this view, all will eventually be welcomed into the kingdom of heaven, even if after a period of refinement by fire. While I do not ultimately agree with its claims, I am hopeful I am somehow wrong. The concept is quite appealing. Certainly, it is more representative of the loving God depicted in Scripture then the traditionalist perspective and it deserves just as much a seat at the table as its competing doctrines. Before closing out this chapter, I will take a brief look at why Universalists find their view compelling.

Philosophy

Immortality of the Soul - For those of a more platonic persuasion, Universal Restoration provides the perfect response to the doctrine of eternal suffering. A soul can be inherently immortal AND unending torture can be averted. While many Universalists acknowledge the reality of a literal hell, they see it only as a place of purification. Ultimately, all are destined to paradise.

God of Love - There is little daylight in philosophies of love between the conditionalist and advocate of Universalism. Both would ardently oppose the view that the God of the Bible is one who is willing to allow his creation to endlessly suffer. The advocate of Universal Restoration may claim superiority here, as she may not be able to tolerate a view of God which does not always sustain life. But I propose there is one problem...

Free Will - Those who hold that man possesses libertarian free will (or the concept that his decisions are made autonomously, outside of divine compulsion) would argue that true love must be the result of a choice. It cannot be forced or simply the result of sin purified away. The Universalist holds that all will eventually turn back to God and suffering will cease. But if libertarian free will is to be maintained, I am not sure where that assurance comes from. It is quite possible at some point, that for the hope of Universalism to be actualized, free will must be removed lest suffering be eternally extended.

Scriptural Support

Advocates of Universalism, as in all three views of the afterlife, find support in Scripture.

A few key verses are referenced below:

*1 Timothy 4:10 - That is why we labor and strive, because we have put our hope in the living God, who is the Savior of all people, and especially of those who believe.

*1 Corinthians 15:21-22 - For since death came through a man, the resurrection of the dead comes also through a man. For as in Adam all die, so in Christ all will be made alive.

*Ephesians 1:7,10 - In him we have redemption through his blood, the forgiveness of sins, in accordance with the riches of God's grace…to be put into effect when the times reach their fulfillment-to bring unity to all things in heaven and on earth under Christ.

For those that hold Scripture in high authority, all three views must wrestle with the synthesis of the passages that seem to contradict what we believe. The conditionalist maintains the wealth of evidence that the wages of sin is eternal death of body and soul makes her position persuasive. There are over three hundred passages in Scripture which use the terms slay, slain, death, die, dies, cut off, kill or killed in describing the judgement of God. And this death is eternal:

*2 Thessalonians 1:9 - They will be punished with everlasting destruction and shut out from the presence of the

Lord and from the glory of his might on the day he comes to be glorified in his holy people and to be marveled at among all those who believe.

*Matthew 25:45-46 - He will reply, "Truly I tell you, whatever you did not do for one of the least of these, you did not do for me." Then they will go away to eternal punishment, but the righteous to eternal life.

Proponents of Universal Restoration, on the other hand, advocate that the Greek word *aionios* has been mistranslated as "eternal" and should rather be interpreted to mean "for an age." They must reconcile this stance with the observation that the same word is used several times in Scripture to reference eternal life (John 6:47, John 10:28, Acts 13:48, Romans 2:7, Romans 5:21; Galatians 6:8) as well as our eternal God (Romans 16:26).

Whatever your persuasion, universalism (Keith Giles has given a much more adequate presentation of this view in Chapter 4), or conditionalism, both doctrines deserve to be strongly considered and both are preferable to the doctrine of eternal suffering.[23]

An End to Eternal Torment

Ultimately, any sound doctrine of hell must both account and advocate for the love of God. A view in which love fails to overcome is one that must be discarded. As presented above, the eternal torment view fails in this regard. It fails to give a sound accounting for the natural mortality of the soul. And it fails to portray hell biblically. It is my hope, and the aim of this present volume, that this doctrine be discarded in light of these grand insufficiencies... lest the *Church* suffer endlessly because of it.

---

23. It is worth noting that conditionalism and universal restoration are not the only alternatives available to those who oppose the doctrine of eternal conscious torment. Later in this volume, Thomas Jay Oord will be presenting what he has called the Relentless Love Theory.

CHAPTER 7

Engaging Gehenna:
Seeing Conditional Immortality
Through the Eyes of Biblical Imagery

Chris Loewen

What is *Gehenna*, the infamous place south of Jerusalem, and why give attention to such a morbid biblical image?[1] Of all the most relevant words that are often translated into English as "hell," *Gehenna* is the only term that is used in Scripture to describe the final fate of the nonbeliever. The term *hadēs* occurs eleven times in the New Testament (Matt 11:23; 16:18; Luke 10:15; 16:23; Acts 2:27; 2:31; 1 Cor. 15:55; Rev. 1:18; 6:8; 20:13, 14). The term *tartaroō* occurs only once (2 Pet 2:4).[2] *Gehenna* is used primarily

1. This chapter is a revision of "Gehenna: The History, Development and Usage of a Common Image for Hell," *Theodidaktos* 13 (2018): 3–12. Thanks to the publisher for granting me permission to incorporate this updated version into this volume. An earlier version of this work was presented at the 2022 Spring Conference of CATA (Canadian American Theological Association). Many thanks to Dr. Dustin Burlet and Dr. Cynthia Westfall who offered their invaluable feedback. Alongside this, I am also indebted to Dr. August Konkel's BI 5101 Hermeneutics course (Providence Theological Seminary) from which certain parts of this work had their original impetus.

2. According to many biblical theologians, all people (believing and unbelieving) go to Sheol or Hades upon death, but only the unbelieving are finally destroyed in Gehenna after the final Resurrection. For more details, see Kim Papaioannou, "Motifs of Death and Hell in the Teaching of Jesus: An examination of Hades Part 1," *Melanesian Journal*

by Jesus in the Gospels (Matt. 5:22, 29, 30; 10:28; 18:9; 23:15, 33; Mark 9:43, 45, 47; Luke 12:5) and once by the Apostle James (3:6). It is conspicuously absent in the writings of Paul and the other works of the New Testament.

The purpose of this chapter is two-fold: (1) to survey the origin, history, and development of *Gehenna* from the Old Testament (OT) to the New Testament (NT), comparing the external evidence seen in the historical rabbinical ideas of *Gehenna* with the internal evidence seen in exclusively biblical development; and (2) to give insight on how this survey informs one's eschatological convictions regarding the final fate of nonbelievers.

The following questions will be addressed in this chapter: What is the eschatological nature of *Gehenna* with respect to the fate of nonbelievers? Does *Gehenna* function primarily as a geographical term, or can we see a development that takes us beyond the basic geographical meaning? Is there any biblical or historical warrant for accepting the popular idea of *Gehenna* as a "garbage dump" just south of Jerusalem, into which the city garbage, and dead bodies of animals and criminals, were thrown to be incinerated? My hope is that the answers to these questions will help further the deconstruction of hell and offer a Conditionalist reconstruction of Gehenna in light of its overall usage throughout the NT.[3]

Origin of Gehenna

The Greek word *Gehenna* is a transliteration of the Hebrew phrase *Ge-hinnom* which, in a handful of variations in the OT, functions primarily as a toponym or "place-name" (Josh.15:8; 18:16; 2 Kings

---

of *Theology* 32 (2016): 103–33. Cf. Fred B. Perason, "Sheol and Hades in Old and New Testament," *Review & Expositor* 35 (1938): 304–14.

3. Conditionalists vary in the way they emphasize God's active vs. passive judgment on the nonbeliever. As a Conditionalist, because of my own Anabaptist leanings, I prefer to emphasize the language of God eventually "removing his life-sustaining power" from those who reject him. For more on this perspective, see Gregory A Boyd, *Crucifixion of the Warrior God: Interpreting the Old Testament's Violent Portraits of God in Light of the Cross* (Minneapolis: Fortress, 2017), 787, 812.

23:10; 2 Chron. 28:3; 33:6; Neh. 11:30; Jer. 7:31, 32; 19:2, 6; 32:35). That is to say, *Ge-hinnom* is a geographical reference to the valley just south of Jerusalem most commonly known as the valley of 'Ben Hinnom.'[4] This place was a "deep and yawning gorge that never [contained] water," and a valley that descended "over six hundred feet from its original source."[5]

Ge-hinnom is used a total of fourteen times in the First Testament: five times it serves as a "purely geographical term" (Josh.15:8 [x2]; 18:16 [x2]; Neh. 11:30); narratively, it is used four times when describing "historical events that happened in the valley and its environs" (2 Kings 23:10; 2 Chron. 28:3; 33:6; Jer. 32:35); lastly, the five remaining occurrences are all within the Jeremaic text as prophecies "about a war in the valley in which God will punish the apostates of Judah" (Jer. 7:31–32 [x2]; 19:2–6 [x3]).[6] In addition to these fourteen specific references, there are also several other OT texts in which the language and imagery of judgment in a valley are used but without direct reference to the actual term *Ge-hinnom* (Isa.30:33; 66:24; Ezek. 39:11–16; Joel 3:1–21). Aside from its geographical usage, each of the above will be examined in turn.

History of *Ge-hinnom*

The valley of Hinnom is the location of some of the darkest moments in Judah's history.[7] Infamously, it came to be known as "the place of child sacrifice."[8] During the reign of King Ahaz (732–716 BC), children were burned alive in the fire as a sacrifice to the god Molech (2 Chron. 28:3; 2 Kings 16:3, 21:6, 33:6). It is written:

---

4. Kim Papaioannou, *The Geography of Hell in the Teaching of Jesus* (Eugene, OR: Pickwick, 2013), 3–4.

5. Edward Fudge, *The Fire That Consumes: A Biblical and Historical Study of the Doctrine of Final Punishment* 3rd ed. (Eugene, OR: Cascade, 2011), 117. This region is now called "Wadi er-Rababi." (*New International Dictionary of New Testament Theology and Exegesis,* ed. Moisés Silva, 2nd edition (Grand Rapids, MI: Zondervan, 2014), s.v. "γέεννα."

6. Papaioannou, *Geography of Hell*, 4.

7. Joachim Jeremias, "γέεννα," *TDNT* 1:657–58.

8. David J. A. Clines, *DCH* 2:343.

"they built high places for Baal in the Valley of Ben Hinnom to sacrifice their sons and daughters to Molech," something YHWH "never commanded, nor did it enter [His] mind, that they should do such a detestable thing and so make Judah sin" (Jer. 32:35).[9] These actions provoked YHWH to foretell of Judah's destruction, an act that would be so devastating "the ears of everyone who hears of it will tingle" (2 Kings 21:12).[10]

Manasseh's grandson Josiah later took the throne. One reads of his sweeping reforms in 2 Kings 23:1–25 (640–609 BC).[11] Josiah led the nation in Israel's reformation. He "desecrated Topheth [the 'fire altar'], which was in the Valley of Ben Hinnom, so [that] no one could use it to sacrifice their son or daughter in the fire to Molech" (v.10).[12] 2 Chronicles also records these events but adds how Josiah took the bones of the dead pagan priests and burned them "on their altars, and so he purged Judah and Jerusalem" of their sin (34:1–7). Regrettably, even though Josiah's pursuit of radical reformation ended the practice of child sacrifices in the *Ge-hinnom* valley, it did not deter the impending destruction soon to befall Judah (cf. 2 Chron. 34:25).[13]

Development of *Ge-hinnom*

The term *Ge-hinnom* is subsequently used in Jeremiah where it is portrayed as a place where the apostate Jews will be completely and utterly destroyed by God. The first instance of *Gehenna* in Jeremiah is 7:29–34 where the LORD tells the prophet of his anger

---

9. Unless otherwise noted, all biblical passages referenced are from the NIV (Grand Rapids, MI: Zondervan, 1984).

10. In the Hebrew: "so that everyone who hears it, his two ears will quiver." See the NET Bible.

11. August H. Konkel, *The NIV Application Commentary: 1 & 2 Kings* (Grand Rapids, MI: Zondervan, 2006).

12. Papaioannou, *Geography of Hell*, 5. Papaioannou further suggests that *Topheth* etymologically means "hearth," "fireplace," or "fire altar." Cf. John Goldingay, *Jeremiah* (Grand Rapids, MI: Eerdmans, 2021), 253–54.

13. For more details see Mark J. Boda, *1–2 Chronicles* (Carol Stream, IL: Tyndale, 2010).

that burns against Judah. There the LORD states: "the people of Judah…have built the high places of Topheth in the Valley of Ben Hinnom to burn their sons and daughters in the fire" (7:30–31). In language of terror and dread, the LORD tells Josiah about the horrible destruction soon to befall Judah. The language of merciless slaughter, and masses of unburied corpses gives the reader the vivid imagery of a bloody "battle scene…and one of utmost desolation."[14]

This language of *Ge-hinnom* is picked up again in Jeremiah 19:1–15, when Jeremiah goes out to the *Ge-hinnom* valley and prophesies directly towards the "kings of Judah and the people of Jerusalem" what he heard from the LORD (19:3a). Jeremiah proclaimed that the "days are coming…when the people will no longer call this place Topheth or the Valley of Ben Hinnom, but a Valley of Slaughter" (19:6). The place where the Israelites killed their innocent infants and young children is where they themselves will now be slaughtered by their enemy's sword.[15]

Considering this background, it is quite likely that the grotesque imagery of a valley filled with dead bodies in Jeremiah 7:29–34 and 19:1–15 would have had a not insignificant impact on the people of Judah who had just recently been a part of Josiah's radical reformation. The prophecy of Jeremiah was a call to repentance lest they and the entire populace of Jerusalem become a valley of slaughter. This call brings to mind the desecrated valley of Hinnom during Josiah's reformation.[16] Shortly after Josiah's death, "Jerusalem fell to the Babylonians and the people of Judah were taken into exile" (2 Kings 25; 2 Chron. 36:15–23).[17]

---

14. Papaioannou, 7.

15. Domeris, *NIDOTTE* 1:1056.

16. Papaioannou, *Geography of Hell*, 9. See also Tremper Longman et al. eds., *Dictionary of Biblical Imagery* (Downers Grove, IL: InterVarsity, 1998), 909–11.

17. Papaioannou, *Geography of Hell*, 8. For further information, see Oded Lipschits, *The Fall and Rise of Jerusalem: Judah under Babylonian Rule* (Winona Lake, IN: Eisenbrauns, 2013).

The final reference of *Ge-hinnom* within the Jeremiah corpus is Jeremiah 31:38–40. This passage is set within the promise of Jerusalem's restoration and the language of the hope of the New Covenant. One day the exiles will return home, Jerusalem will be rebuilt, and God will dwell with His people once again—even the valley where the "corpses and ashes" (cf. 7:30–34) were thrown are declared "sacred for Yahweh."[18] Bradley Jersak opines that because Jeremiah moves from judgment to hope, it suggests possible proof of universal salvation.[19] To extrapolate a universalist vision from Jeremiah remains difficult, however, when one notes the prophet returns to judgment in chapters 46–51; the message in 31:38–40 is simply that "the future of the exiles was not to languish in exile forever…and the city will never [again] be uprooted or demolished."[20] The destruction of Jerusalem in 70 AD further suggests that the ultimate fulfillment of this prophecy should be found elsewhere, i.e., the New Jerusalem (Rev. 21—22).[21]

By far the clearest allusion to the Valley of *Ge-hinnom* outside of Jeremiah is Isaiah 66:24, which happens to be the *Ge-hinnom* text that Jesus references the most in the gospels. Contextually, Isaiah 66:1–24 is describing an eschatological battle scene outside of Jerusalem.[22] The LORD protects the righteous within the city while utterly slaying the wicked who rebel against him, by divine fire and sword (Isa. 66:15–16).

It is written: the righteous "will go out and look upon the dead bodies" of the wicked, lying just outside of Jerusalem, where "their

---

18. Goldingay, *Jeremiah*, 660–62.

19. Bradley Jersak, *Her Gates Will Never Be Shut: Hope, Hell, and the New Jerusalem* (Eugene, OR: Wipf & Stock, 2009), 63–66.

20. Christopher J. H. Wright, *Jeremiah* (Downers Grove, IL: InterVarsity, 2014), 333–34. Goldingay (*Jeremiah*, 662) cheekily states, "If only it were the case that the city had not been pulled up or smashed again ever!"

21. Wright, *Jeremiah*, 339.

22. Daniel I. Block, "The Old Testament on Hell," in *Hell under Fire: Modern Scholarship Reinvents Eternal Punishment*, eds. Christopher W. Morgan and Robert A. Peterson (Grand Rapids, MI: Zondervan, 2004), 60-61.

worm does not die" and the "fire is not quenched" (Isa. 66:24). The *Ge-hinnom* Valley is not mentioned in this text, but the imagery has some noteworthy connections with Jeremiah: a great battle resulting in massive loss of life, where the dead are left unburied and left to the consumption by scavengers.[23]

Subsequent to Jeremiah, we do not hear of *Ge-hinnom* again in the rest of the OT.[24] There are other allusions to destruction in a valley within OT texts such as Isaiah 30:33, Ezekiel 39:11–16, and Joel 3:1–21, but in each of these cases (as seen with Isaiah 66:24), *Ge-hinnom* is not mentioned by name. "This can only mean that the word *Ge-hinnom* had not yet developed into a byword for the punishment that God would inflict on the wicked in the eschatological future."[25] It seems to be the case, then, that *Ge-hinnom* in the OT was a term only used in pre-exilic texts.

The Silence of *Gehenna*

Interestingly, the Septuagint "does not have *Gehenna* and Josephus mentions neither the term nor the matter."[26] Within the Second Temple literature leading up to the time of Christ, it is questionable that *Gehenna* was ever used as a toponym for final punishment.[27] Kim Papaioannou suggests that the relevant mentions of *Gehenna* in the Apocrypha and Pseudepigrapha are found in the later writings of 4 *Ezra*, 2 *Baruch*, *Apocalypse of Abraham*, and the *Sibylline*

---

23. Fudge, 76.

24. Domeris, *NIDOTTE* 1:1055–57. However, we do see *Gehenna* show up in the Targums a good hand full of times. Most relevant to this study is Targum Isaiah 66:24, "And they will come out and see the bodies of the sinful men who rebelled against My Memra, for their breaths will not die, and their fire will not be extinguished, and they will be judging the wicked in Gehenna until the righteous say to them, 'We have seen enough.'" For more details, see Bruce D. Chilton (ed.), *The Aramaic Bible: The Isaiah Targum* (Collegeville, MN: Liturgical, 1987), 128.

25. Papaioannou, 12.

26. Jeremias, γέεννα," *TDNT* 1:657–58.

27. Papaioannou, 12–20.

Oracles. All of these, he avers, "are dated after AD 70, toward the end of the [first] century or even later."[28]

There is, therefore, a large gap between the *Ge-hinnom* of Jeremaic origin and the *Gehenna* of the later first century AD. *Gehinnom*, according to Jeremiah, was a valley that would have conjured up explicit images of slaughter, death, and (complete and utter) devastation and annihilation. According to later Jewish writings, *Gehenna* became specific and intensely eschatological term referring to an otherworldly place, where "the wicked, sometimes in their bodies, sometimes only as disembodied souls, are sometimes annihilated, but often anguish in fire forever without end."[29] In other words, Jeremiah's *Gehenna* images annihilation, but later Jewish writings imagine *Gehenna* as a place of eternal torment. But how did one lead to the other?

It is difficult to reconcile these ideas when there is such a large historical gap with no evidence showing "a coherent, gradual development of the theme beginning with Jeremiah and continuing down the centuries."[30] That the Gehenna tradition suddenly developed from the language of death and destruction in the OT to the otherworldly place of eternal conscious torment is unwarranted; the burden of proof seems to be on those who maintain otherwise.

---

28. Papaioannou, 19. The early sections of Sibylline Oracles Books 1 & 2, and the Rabbinic Traditions of Yohannan b. Zakkai (b.Ber.4.2 and t.San.13.4) are also sometimes claimed as pre-70 AD, but that is not conclusive. Papaioannou suggest it is more likely to be from post 70 AD and into the early 2nd century. The same can be said of the Mishnah and Babylonian Talmud. In these writings, "the word Gehenna appears well over fifty times," with a few rabbis being the earliest attributions in the later part of the first century AD. But in most cases, Papaioannou suggests that "they are attributed to Rabbis of the third and fourth centuries." For an excellent survey of later Jewish writings and their influence on the doctrine of final punishment, see Glenn Peoples, "Worms and Fire: The Rabbis or Isaiah?" in *Rethinking Hell: Exploring Evangelical Conditionalism.* August 17, 2012. Accessed December 4, 2017. http://www.rethinkinghell.com/2012/08/worms-and-fire-the-rabbis-or-isaiah/#identifier_9_1348. See also, David Instone-Brewer, "Eternal Punishment in First-Century Jewish Thought," in *A Consuming Passion: Essays on Hell and Immortality in Honor of Edward Fudge*, eds. Christopher M. Date and Ron Highfield (Eugene, OR: Pickwick, 2015).

29. Papaioannou, 22.

30. Papaioannou, 21.

This is not to dismiss the fact that there were some texts in the intertestamental period, albeit few and in embryonic form, that warn of eternal torment. But they were not in connection with the geographical *Gehenna*. Rather, they appear to have sprung forth from non-Jewish philosophy.[31] Based on the evidence at hand, it seems likely that Jesus, in his teaching on Hell, is the first to resurrect *Gehenna* from its hiding place to continue the *Gehenna* motif of Jeremiah.[32]

Advent of Gehenna

As noted above, *Gehenna* is mentioned a total of twelve times, eleven times from the lips of Jesus (Matt 5:22, 29, 30; 10:28; 18:9; 23:15, 33; Mark 9:43, 45, 47; Luke 12:5). "Twice he addresses the Pharisees. All else that Jesus says about hell is directed to his own disciples."[33] Clearly, Matthew uses *Gehenna* most generously.[34] As indicated elsewhere, the only other NT occurrence of *Gehenna* is in James 3:6.[35] The understanding of *Gehenna* in the NT, especially in the Gospels, is that it is the location where the wicked are punished after the final resurrection.[36] In most cases, according to Louw & Nida, the term "is rendered as 'place of punishment' or

---

31. Fudge, 96–97, 116–20.

32. Papaioannou, 25.

33. Fudge, 286.

34. Papaioannou, 23.

35. The NET Bible states, "The word translated hell is "Gehenna" (γέεννα, *geenna*), a Greek transliteration of the Hebrew words *ge hinnom* ("Valley of Hinnom"). This was the valley along the south side of Jerusalem. In OT times it was used for human sacrifices to the pagan god Molech (cf. Jer. 7:31; 19:5–6; 32:35), and it came to be used as a place where human excrement and rubbish were disposed of and burned. In the intertestamental period, it came to be used symbolically as the place of divine punishment (cf. 1 En. 27:2; 90:26; 4 Ezra 7:36)."

36. Walter Bauer, *A Greek-English Lexicon of the New Testament and Other Early Christian Literature*, 2nd ed. (Chicago: University of Chicago Press, 1979), 153.

'place where the dead suffer' or 'place where the dead suffer because of their sins.'"[37]

Among the *Gehenna* Gospel references, it is interesting to recognize the unique emphasis on the body, i.e., there is language of mutilated body parts in Matt 5:29–30, 18:9 and Mark 9:43–48 with *Gehenna* as the context. For example, Mark 9:43 states: "If your hand causes you to sin, cut it off. It is better for you to enter life maimed than with two hands to go into *Gehenna*."

Jesus repeats this phrase twice when he speaks similarly of feet and eyes (vv. 45–46). As a parallel between a partial loss and a total loss, Jesus seems to be pointing out that to enter life mutilated is better than being a dead corpse thrown into *Gehenna*. What is more, almost akin to spiritual gangrene, if action is not taken to get rid of sin, it will eventually consume and kill the whole body.[38] A comparison is drawn via the severed limb and the lifeless body in Gehenna.

A corpse thrown into *Gehenna* is reminiscent of the dead bodies in Jeremiah's Valley of Slaughter and Isaiah's scene of massacre (Jer. 7:32; 19:6; Isa. 66:24). Here we notice that Jesus, a Jewish rabbi immersed in the Hebrew Scriptures, i.e., the First Testament (OT), quotes directly from Isaiah 66:24. Then, by inserting *Gehenna* in his quotation, he marries Jeremiah's Gehenna with Isaiah's valley. The images complement each other. All of these "depict [gruesome] battle scenes that result in a devastation of mutilated and *dead* bodies."[39] Furthermore, the marriage of these ideas suggests the eschatological reality of *Gehenna*. Focusing on the language of Isaiah

---

37. Johannes P. Louw and Eugene A. Nida, eds., *Greek English Lexicon of the New Testament Based on Semantic Domains* (New York: United Bible Societies, 1988), 295.

38. William L. Lane, *The Gospel According to Mark* (Grand Rapids, MI: Eerdmans, 1974), 348. See Matt. 5:27–30. While Mark emphasizes the "cutting off the hand" (9:43), with no further explanation, Matthew goes further by saying, "…and throw it away" (5:29, 30). See also Luke 12:4–5 and the distinction drawn between the "body" (*sōma*) and the "soul" (*psuchē*). For further information, consult the standard commentaries.

39. Papaioannou, 22 (emphasis mine). As to the language of "unquenchable fire" (irresistible fire) and "undying worms/maggots" see Ezekiel 20:47–48; Amos 5:5–6; Matthew 3:12.

66:24, Traditionalists curiously repeat their fixation with the image of unending fire and worm but skim over the explicit image of the "dead bodies" that are the very subjects of destruction. When one observes Jesus' marriage of Jeremiah's Gehenna and Isaiah's valley, the result seems to suggest death and destruction as the controlling motif, not eternal torment.[40]

In addition to the emphasis on the body in the gospels is the "geographical dimension in the development of the *Gehenna* motif."[41] Not only is *Gehenna* a geographical term, but it is also a thoroughly Jewish term, one that Jews in Jesus' day would have understood as part of their history. Mark and Luke use the term sparingly (might this be explained, perhaps, by their majority Gentile audience?).[42] James, like Matthew, was also addressing a primarily Jewish readership.[43] Outside these incidences, there are no other NT references to the geographical *Gehenna*. Understandably, to a Gentile who was unfamiliar with the geography and history of Jerusalem, the teachings of Jesus and the OT, the term *Gehenna* may have had little impact.[44]

This may, perhaps, seem to explain the absence of *Gehenna* in the writings of Paul, who does not speak of the fate of the wicked in geographical language akin to Jesus or the other apostles. One could argue that it would not have made sense for him to do so,

---

40. Among Traditionalists, there are differing views. Many believe in a form of "separationism" which is a Metaphorical view of Hell. Along with this is a form of "Lewisianism" in which all who are in hell choose it, and the door is locked from the inside (C.S. Lewis, *The Great Divorce*). Yet there are those, like N.T. Wright, who suggest a kind of "Dehumanizationism," that those who refuse to respond to the gospel, and only worship themselves, "that after death they become at last, by their own effective choice, beings that once were human but now are not," but however, he admits that this is wandering into "territory that no one can claim to have mapped" (N.T. Wright, *Surprised by Hope*, 182–83). To illustrate this, some point to Smeagol's ghastly transformation into Gollum in the *Lord of the Rings* Trilogy. Yet, ironically, Gollum himself is eventually annihilated in the volcanic fires of Mount Doom.

41. Papaioannou, 23.

42. Fudge, 117.

43. Ibid.

44. Papaioannou, 23. See also Lane, 348–49.

since he was writing to a mixed audience in Asia Minor who would not have understood such geography.[45]

Instead of geography, Paul uses language of *teleology* that emphasize destruction and death. Said differently, Paul is interested in the decisive or punctiliar act of destruction as the end (*telos*) of the unregenerate. To put it yet another way, Paul is not interested in the "how" but the "fact" of destruction. The apostle is interested in the natural consequences and outcome of ones' present decisions. Paul uses a wide variety of words to communicate this but the five most common are: (1) *apollumi* (Rom. 14:15; 1 Cor. 8:11; 10:9–10); (2) *apōleia* (Rom. 9:22–24; Phil 1:28; 3:18–19; 2 Thess. 2:3,8; 1 Tim. 6:9); (3) *olethros* (1 Cor. 5:5; 1 Thess. 5:3; 2 Thess. 1:8–9; 1 Tim. 6:9); (4) *phtheirō* (1 Cor. 3:17); (5) *phthora* (Gal. 6:7).[46] Three examples that highlight the language of *teleology* clearly are Philippians 3:18–19, 2 Thessalonians 1:9, and 1 Timothy 6:9. In Philippians, Paul declares that those who live as "enemies of the cross" will find "their end (*telos*) is destruction (*apōleia*)" (Phil 3:18–19).[47] In 2 Thessalonians, on the Day of the LORD, the nonbeliever will be punished with "eternal destruction (*olethros*) from the presence of the LORD" (2 Thess. 1:9).[48] In 1 Timothy, Paul warns the person "desiring to be rich" that greed "plunges people into ruin (*olethros*) and destruction (*apōleia*)" (1 Tim. 6:9).[49]

---

45. In a private conversation, J. Richard Middleton pointed out to me that "different contexts (and conceptual training, etc.) lead different people to use different ideas/images, etc. to communicate the same basic idea."

46. For more information see Silva, *NIDNTTE* 1:357–61; 3:485–88; 4:597–602.

47. Gordon D. Fee, *Paul's Letter to the Philippians* (Grand Rapids, MI: Eerdmans, 1995).

48. For more information, see Daniel G. Reid, "2 Thessalonians 1:9: 'Separated from' or 'Destruction from' the Presence of the Lord?" (presentation, ETS Pauline Studies Group, Colorado Springs, CO, November 16, 2001), 1–18.

49. For an excellent study on Paul's language of destruction as dependent upon the LXX, see Nicholas Rudolph Quient, "Destruction from the Presence of the Lord: Paul's Intertextual Use of the LXX in 2 Thess. 1:9" (presentation, Rethinking Hell Conference, London, UK, October 7-8, 2016), 1–24. Nicholas Quient helpfully points out, "the conjunction *kai*, which is in between the two nouns [*olethros* and *apōleia*], could be taken epexegetically, that is, creating an intentional rhetorical redundancy ('destruction, annihilation') and using the second as an intensifier (cf. hendiadys)" (12). Cf. Stanley E. Porter, *Idioms of the Greek New Testament*—revised edition (Sheffield Academic Press, 1992).

Paul repeatedly uses *non-geographical* language whenever he speaks of the fate of the unbeliever.[50]

To summarize the evidence of *Gehenna* language in the NT, it may be said that Jesus stands much "closer to the original source of the Gehenna tradition," and that his references to *Gehenna* "have a coherence that reflects a unified source."[51]

Speaking plainly, while Jesus invokes the *Gehenna* of Jeremaic origin and Paul affirms the language associated with *Gehenna*, Paul moves beyond the geographic language of *Gehenna* to a more clear *teleological* language that emphasizes destruction and death as the *end* of the unbeliever. However, as we move further away from Jesus and Paul into the later Jewish writings, we see a tendency to move further away from "the body towards an interest in disembodied souls," which reveals a lack of unity on the consensus of *Gehenna*.[52]

---

50. Peter Grice, "Annihilation In 2 Thessalonians 1:9 (Part 1): Destroyed by the Glory of His Manifest Presence," *Rethinking Hell*, November 14, 2016, http://www.rethinking-hell.com/2016/11/annihilation-in-2-thessalonians-19-part-1-destroyed-by-the-glory-of-his-manifest-presence; and Ronnie Demler and William Tanksley Jr., "Annihilation In 2 Thessalonians 1:9 (Part 2): Separation Or Obliteration?—The Present Controversy," *Rethinking Hell*, December 5, 2016, http://www.rethinkinghell.com/2016/12/annihilation-in-2-thess-1-9-part-2-separation-or-obliteration/. Cf. Charles L. Quarles, "The ἀπό of 2 Thess. 1:9 and the Nature of Eternal Punishment," *WTJ* 59 (1997), 201-11; Nicholas Rudolph Quient, "Paul and the Annihilation of Death," in *A Consuming Passion,* ed. Christopher M. Date and Ron Highfield (Wipf & Stock, 2015), 98–102.

51. Papaioannou, 24. The curious reader might wonder why, in this study, there is no mention of the Lake of Fire and the Second Death (Rev. 20:10–15) and their relation to *Gehenna*. Within the Old and New Testaments there is no explicit connection made between these images, and since Revelation is of a different genre, it would require another paper to map out those connections. There is one incidence where these images are paired in the text of Targum Psalm 49:11. See "Rethinking Hell Live 061: Hell and the Book of Revelation, with William Tanksley," https://www.youtube.com/watch?v=vMGn-lublGzM. For more information, see Christopher M. Date and William Tanksley Jr., "This is the Second Death, the Lake of Fire," forthcoming.

52. Papaioannou, 24. For more on the development of the language of the soul see Luke Jeffery Janssen, *Soul Searching: The Evolution of Judeo-Christian Thinking on the Soul and the Afterlife* (Eugene, OR: Wipf & Stock, 2019). Cf. Tröger, "*psuchē*," *TDNT* 9:608–60.

Gehenna as a Garbage Dump?

Foremost among the modern ideas surrounding *Gehenna* is that of a smoldering garbage dump south of Jerusalem where perpetual fires consumed the city waste and the dead bodies of criminals thrown into it. Many prominent scholars appeal to this idea, and often without evidence or explanation.[53] R. T. France in his commentary on the Greek text seems to be driven by this assumption.[54] Curiously, even the eminent Louw & Nida lexicon appeals to this notion.[55]

It seems that most people understand that during Josiah's sweeping reformation (when he declared the valley unclean) it was subsequently "used for burning refuse and the bodies of criminals."[56] Supposedly, this was then an ongoing practice that continued into Jesus' day where the "sight and smell of the place" would have been familiar to the contemporary Jew.[57] Thus, according to many advocates of this idea who are Traditionalists, Jesus is using the garbage dump as a metaphor for Hell as a place of eternal conscious torment.[58]

The idea of *Gehenna* as a municipal garbage dump, however, is based on thin evidence.[59] Among the scholars who question this

---

53. Examples include N. T. Wright, *Matthew For Everyone: Part 1* (Louisville, KY: Westminster John Knox, 2004), 211–12; Robert A. Morey, *Death and the Afterlife* (Minneapolis, MN: Bethany, 1984), 87–88.

54. R. T. France, *The Gospel of Mark* (Grand Rapids, MI: Eerdmans, 2002), 379–85.

55. Louw & Nida, 295.

56. Silva, *NIDNTTE* 1:548.

57. Block, "The Old Testament on Hell," 60–61.

58. In his criticism of the Traditionalist interpretation of Mark 9:42–48, France states: "The wording of this pericope does not in itself settle the question either way, quite apart from the danger of using vivid traditional imagery to establish formal doctrine" (*The Gospel of Mark*, 382).

59. See for instance: John Stackhouse, "Terminal Punishment," in *Four Views on Hell*, 2nd ed., ed. Preston Sprinkle (Grand Rapids, MI: Zondervan, 2016), 63. Other scholars who express hesitance with the garbage dump motif include: James A. Montgomery, "The Holy City and Gehenna," *Journal of Biblical Literature* 27 (1908): 34; R. T. France, *The Gospel of Matthew* (Grand Rapids, MI: Eerdmans, 2007), 202; Robert W. Yarbrough, "Jesus on Hell," in *Hell Under Fire*, 79; Christopher W. Morgan, "Biblical Theology: Three Pictures of Hell," in *Hell Under Fire*, 146; Denny Burk, "Eternal Conscious Torment," in *Four Views on Hell*, 22–23.

theory, Francis Chan and Preston Sprinkle are helpful in pointing out "just because Jesus' description of hell may have been inspired by the image of a burning garbage dump (if it was), doesn't
mean that He is referring to the actual garbage dump when he
uses the word *Gehenna*."[60] To suggest that Jesus is referring to an
actual garbage dump in geographic terms is to (grossly?) misunder-
stand his teaching(s). Chan and Sprinkle effectively illustrate this
misunderstanding:

> I've often heard people refer to a gridlocked freeway as a
> parking lot. The statement is inspired by a literal parking
> lot, but nobody is claiming that people drive to the free-
> way, stop, lock their cars, and then go about their business.
> That's just the way imagery works.[61]

Within linguistic studies, D. A. Carson refers to this as confusing the "referent with the sense."[62] Papaioannou points out that
the garbage dump motif is in awkward tension with Luke 12:4–5
which draws a contrast between "humans who can kill and then do
nothing more [and] God who can kill and then cast into Gehenna.
If indeed there was a fire burning in the literal valley of *Ge-hinnom*,
the contrast loses its power—not only God, but humans can also
cast into *Gehenna*."[63]

Even when we set aside the functionality of languages, G. R.
Beasley-Murray asserts, "The notion...that the city's rubbish was
burned in this valley, has no further basis than a statement by the
Jewish scholar [David] Kimhi (sic) made about A.D. 1200; it is

---

60. Francis Chan and Preston M. Sprinkle, *Erasing Hell: What God Said about Eternity
and the Things We Made Up* (Colorado Springs, CO: David C. Cook, 2011), 59.

61. Chan and Sprinkle, 59.

62. D. A. Carson, *Exegetical Meaning: An Introduction to Lexical Semantics*, Revised
Edition (Grand Rapids, MI: Zondervan, 1994), 101–18. For even more details, see
Benjamin Baxter, "Hebrew and Greek Word-Study Fallacies," *MJTM* 12 (2010–2011),
3–32 alongside Baxter, "The Meaning of Biblical Words," *MJTM* 11 (2009–2010):
89–120.

63. Papaioannou, 6.

not attested in any ancient source."[64] David Kimhi, a medieval rabbi, wrote in his commentary on Psalm 27: "Gehenna is a repugnant place, into which filth and cadavers are thrown, and in which fires perpetually burn in order to consume the filth and bones, on which account, by analogy, the judgment of the wicked is called 'Gehenna.'"[65] Somewhat ironic is the earliest source of this garbage dump allusion when we notice that Kimhi who was writing "from Europe, by the way, not Israel" himself only saw it as an "analogy" for "the judgment of the wicked."[66]

Peter Head is even more terse when he explicates that, within the primary sources and ancient texts, the evidence for the existence of *Gehenna* as a "fiery rubbish dump in this location" is nonexistent, but "in any case, a thorough investigation would be appreciated."[67] Furthermore, as an archeologist, Bailey points out that there is no evidence for *Gehenna* as a garbage dump in the "archeological data from the intertestamental or rabbinic periods."[68]

If *Gehenna* was a fiery garbage dump just south of Jerusalem, we would "be able to dig around and find evidence."[69] But there is none. Gehenna did not become "infamous as a flaming heap of garbage." Rather, it is an explicit reference to the Jeremaic Valley of Slaughter where God severely judged the nation of Judah.[70] How is it that the majority of the Christian evangelical churches have adopted an idea of *Gehenna* that has no evidence earlier than 1200 AD, hundreds and hundreds of years after Jesus' earthly ministry?

---

64. G. R. Beasley-Murray, *Jesus and the Kingdom of God* (Grand Rapids, MI: Eerdmans, 1986), 376–77n.92.

65. As cited in Lloyd R. Bailey, "Gehenna: The Topography of Hell," *Biblical Archaeologist* 49, no. 3 (September 1968): 188.

66. Chan and Sprinkle, 60, italics mine.

67. Peter M. Head, "The Duration of Divine Judgment in the New Testament," in *Eschatology in Bible & Theology: Evangelical Essays at the Dawn of a New Millennium*, eds. Kent E. Brower and Mark W. Elliott (Downers Drove, IL: InterVarsity, 1997), 223.

68. Bailey, "Gehenna: The Topography of Hell," 189.

69. Chan and Sprinkle, *Erasing Hell*, 59.

70. Burk, "Eternal Conscious Torment," in *Four Views on Hell*, 22–23.

Conclusion

Gehenna has an unavoidable relationship to the *Ge-hinnom* of Jeremiah where the apostate Jews were utterly slaughtered and left unburied and exposed to the elements and scavengers. Beyond Jeremiah's usage of *Ge-hinnom,* it does not appear anywhere else in the OT until Jesus incorporates it into his teaching of the fate of the wicked in the NT. Jesus seems to continue the *Gehenna* motif of Jeremiah by focusing on the body and bringing in the imagery of Isaiah 66:24, thereby giving a stark image of appalling destruction where the unbelievers are completely and utterly destroyed and annihilated.

To be sure, the Jewish hearer would have understood Jesus' geography in a rather plain and straightforward manner and knew the valley of which Jesus was speaking of. But what is helpful to note is that *Gehenna* can be considered a partial vision (a type if you would), of the fuller judgment anticipated for the whole world, and indeed the entire cosmos.[71] In other words, what is true of the Jewish *Gehenna* in its geographical sense is true of the cosmos when God finally comes to destroy all evil. Locality is always part of a punctiliar act of destruction, but what is the focus of Jesus and Paul, and the other NT writers?

It seems to be the case, therefore, that given their particular contexts and environs from which they wrote, stress is placed on the *act* rather than the *location* of destruction. As such, Hell is not merely a place one goes to, but most importantly, it is the *telos,* the natural consequences of choosing a life apart from God. In the language of Conditional Immortality, Hell is when the offer of life is forever removed from their reach.

---

71. For more on "typology" see: James M. Hamilton, *Typology: Understanding the Bible's Promise-Shaped Patterns: How Old Testament Expectations are Fulfilled in Christ* (Zondervan Academic, 2022); Kenneth Berding and Jonathan Lunde, eds. *Three Views on the New Testament Use of the Old Testament* (Zondervan Academic, 2008).

CHAPTER 8

God's Glory as Relentless Love

Thomas Jay Oord

Of all the arguments for hell, the one I find most puzzling says hell glorifies God. How can everlasting torment give God glory?!

Christians aligned with the Westminster Confession are most likely to argue this. One sentence in the Confession states the case: "By the decree of God, for the manifestation of His glory, some men and angels are predestined unto everlasting life, and others foreordained to everlasting death."

At the Confession's conclusion, we get a clearer picture of how hell allegedly glorifies God. A judgment day was appointed "for the manifestation of the glory of His mercy in the eternal salvation of the elect and of His justice in the damnation of the reprobate, who are wicked and disobedient... The wicked, who know not God, and obey not the gospel of Jesus Christ, shall be cast into eternal torment, and punished with everlasting destruction from the presence of the Lord, and from the glory of His power." God is allegedly glorified by decreeing some to "eternal torment," "everlasting destruction," or "everlasting death."

My theological intuitions differ from the Westminster Confession. Those intuitions and the logic of love lead me to reject the idea God condemns anyone to everlasting punishment. The biggest differences derive from my alternate understandings of God's power and love.

My view of God's glory prompts me to deconstruct hell.

In this essay, I do at least two things. First, I question the logic of thinking everlasting torment—the common view of hell—brings God glory. Second, I offer an alternative view of the afterlife. It claims God's love is both uncontrolling and relentless.

Hell Glorifies God?

For a contemporary advocate of the idea that hell manifests God's glory, I did a Google search for "hell glorifies God" and took the highest ranking article. It was titled, "How Does Hell Glorify God?"[1] The piece is by Jim Hamilton, Professor of Biblical Theology at The Southern Baptist Theological Seminary, one of the largest seminaries in America.

Hamilton begins his article with what he calls "The Bible's Big Story." God spoke the world into being and "set the terms," he says. Life now follows God's pre-decided plot. In the end, God will "consign [the wicked] to everlasting punishment" and "take those who believed the word of God and the testimony of Jesus into a new, better, perfect place."

The point of hell, says Hamilton, is that God keeps his word. "That God sends the wicked to hell shows God to be faithful and just… If he does not send the wicked to hell, he has not upheld his own righteous standard and he has not been just."

Hamilton's reasoning for how hell glorifies God claims the righteous are ultimately proven right. "Hell vindicates those who obey God's terms," he says, "even if they suffered terribly for doing so. Hell vindicates the righteous who were persecuted by the wicked. Hell glorifies God."

---

1. Jim Hamilton, "How Does Hell Glorify God?," *9Marks Journal* (August 20, 2010) https://www.9marks.org/article/how-does-hell-glorify-god/

Crucial to this argument is the belief a sovereign God initially set the terms for mercy and justice. God must stay faithful to those terms, which say the unrighteous will be punished in hell and the righteous given eternal life. God is glorified, therefore, if God stays true to an arrangement God alone decided.

One wonders why God didn't at the outset set terms that provide eternal bliss to all. Why didn't God decide to be merciful and forgive everyone? Wouldn't this be more loving? And more glorious?

Hamilton realizes some perceive his scenario as troublesome. "How seriously should we take those who object to hell," he asks, "or try to rewrite the story so that hell isn't part of it?" Hamilton answers his own question: "As seriously as we would take Hamlet critiquing Shakespeare's work. Hamlet has no independent existence. He can only critique Shakespeare if the author decides to write that scene."

In this analogy, Hamilton portrays creatures as having no will of their own. God is the author who controls the characters he writes into existence, including foreordaining their ultimate fate. This means God predetermined some would not repent, and they cannot do other than what God pre-decided. Hamilton seems untroubled by this, because he assumes God is all-controlling.

In a summary section, Hamilton repeats his key points. "Hell glorifies God," he says, because it shows that God "keeps his word," "demonstrates God's power to subdue all," "shows how unspeakably merciful he is to those who trust him," "visits justice against those who reject God," and "vindicates all who suffer."

Remarkably absent from this defense of hell is the category of forgiveness. Rather than forgiving all people, the God whom Hamilton affirms only forgives those who trust in him. Rather than calling the righteous to forgive those who harm, God vindicates them by punishing their opponents. Hamilton's God gets revenge rather than reconciles. And God pre-decides it all.

If this is divine love, I respond, I want nothing to do with it! Call me rebellious if you like. Rather than glorify God, Hamilton's view portrays God as controlling, limited in forgiveness, and bent on tormenting some in hell everlastingly. That's not love!

If hell glorifies God, divine glory be damned!

The Bible Says Hell Glorifies God?

Those who think hell glorifies God appeal to the Bible. Romans 9 is often marshalled to support their claims. The key passages are verses 22-24, but a quick overview of the chapter seems necessary.

Some read Romans 9 as saying God sovereignly predestines all that occurs. They point to passages that speak of God loving Jacob but hating Esau, God hardening Pharoah's heart, and a potter (God) determining the clay's use. Although Paul's overall arguments in the book of Romans appeal to creaturely freedom to choose salvation, predestinarians think God alone decides the fate of everyone.[2]

The point of Romans 9, however, is not the predestination of each person. It's an argument for why God includes those outside Israel. God uses negative actions—Esau's, Pharaoh's, or those who reject Paul's message—to bring about something positive. God is squeezing good from the bad God didn't want in the first place.[3] As God wrings something right from what was wrong, God invites those outside Israel to a loving relationship.

In this context we find Romans 9:22-24, the passage often used to claim hell glorifies God. I'll cite the New International Version translation:

> What if God, although choosing to show his wrath and make his power known, bore with great patience the objects

---

2. "Predestination" can be understood in various ways. In this essay, I'll use the word to refer to a Calvinist view that says God predestines some to damnation.

3. For what I call this "didactic" dimension to solving the problem of evil, see Thomas Jay Oord, *God Can't: How to Believe in God and Love after Tragedy, Abuse, and Other Evils* (Grasmere, ID: SacraSage, 2019), ch. 4, and *Pluriform Love: An Open and Relational Theology of Well-Being* (Grasmere, ID: SacraSage, 2022), ch. 6.

of his wrath—prepared for destruction? What if he did this to make the riches of his glory known to the objects of his mercy, whom he prepared in advance for glory—even us, whom he also called, not only from the Jews but also from the Gentiles?

Paul is asking a series of rhetorical questions to make an argument. The key line allegedly related to hell is "bore with great patience the objects of his wrath—prepared for destruction." Those who think hell glorifies God interpret this to mean God prepared some for damnation and others for heaven.

The key to making sense of this passage is to see the differences between the verbs translated "prepared" in verses 22 and 23. The first (*katartizo*) is passive, and it has no subject. It does *not* say God does the preparing. Rather than a reference to hell, it is better understood as referring to natural negative consequences. Sin is destructive; it reaps negative consequences.

The second verb translated "prepared" (*proetoimazo*) is active. This *is* something God does. Because of everlasting mercy, God prepares in advance the glory that comes from love.[4] References to divine glory in this passage, therefore, refer to God's mercy in calling both Jews and Gentiles. It does not refer to God's predestining some for hell.

The main point: divine glory is revealed when God "bore with great patience" the harm that sin causes.

The "wrath" Paul mentions in this passage refers to God's anger, not divine punishment. God gets angry when we hurt ourselves, one another, and the earth. Sin destroys. Despite being angry at sin's destructiveness, says Paul, God remains patient.

Paul's convoluted sentences muddy our interpretive waters. If I were translating the passage, it would be something like this:

---

4. On the importance of the two Greek verbs and their tenses, see Ben Witherington III, *Paul's Letter to the Romans: A Socio-Rhetorical Commentary* (Grand Rapids, MI: Eerdmans, 2004), 258.

What if God, although angry at the destruction that sin causes and although powerful, is patient? What if God is patient even though angry at the destructiveness sin causes? What if this patience displays the riches of divine glory, the glory of God's everlasting love for everyone God calls, which is all of us, Jew and Gentile?

Paul refers to divine glory by saying God's loving patience should amaze us. Despite sin, evil, and destruction, God patiently and mercifully calls all to love.

Merciful patience—not hell—reveals God's glory.

For How Long is God Patient?

"Okay, God is patient," I can imagine a reader saying. "But for how long is God patient? Maybe hell is evidence that God's patience has limits."

"What if God's patience is everlasting?" I might respond.

"Interesting," the reader might say. "What would everlasting patience look like?"

"I'll explain in a moment," I might say. "But first let me ask a question, Which do you find more glorious?

1) The idea God sends some to hell and others to heaven.

2) the idea God patiently woos everyone to the possibility of eternal happiness?"

"That's easy," the reader might reply. "I'm more in awe of a God who works patiently for the happiness of all!"

"Welcome to the logic of love," I respond.

Alternative Views of the Afterlife

Once we set aside the idea that hell glorifies God, at least three alternative views of the afterlife offer themselves for consideration. I'll argue for the superiority of a view I call "Relentless Love." But I first want to explore the other two briefly.

Annihilation

One alternative to thinking God sends people to hell is the view God annihilates the wicked. This view says a loving God sends no one to never-ending torment. Instead, God destroys the unrepentant. God either annihilates them in a display of flashing omnipotence or passively by not sustaining their lives. God causes or allows the eradication of the unrighteous.

This view is often called "annihilationism" but sometimes "conditionalism." It takes literally biblical statements that say fire consumes the wicked (e.g., Heb. 6:8, 10:7; 12:29) or passages that talk of the wicked being destroyed (Matt. 7:13). Some argue unloving people cannot persist in the presence of pure love.

In the annihilation view, afterlife existence is conditioned upon God's sovereign decision to keep us alive. But God exterminates some people, giving them no second chances. If these sinners wanted to repent later, it's too late. Like Jim Hamilton's God, this deity sets up the rules and judges all according to them.

As I see it, the annihilation view rightly says actions have consequences and our decisions matter. It rightly says God sends no one to never-ending torment. But the annihilation view assumes God quits on some people. God grows impatient and gives up, failing to forgive and offer another chance.

In the annihilation view, God's patience has limits.

By contrast, I believe a God of everlasting love never gives up. On anyone, ever. God doesn't say, "I gave her 264,837 chances to repent, but no more!" Nor does God say, "I'd rather destroy him than forgive."

The relentless love view says God *always* forgives. God turns the other cheek—in this life and the next. The steadfast love of the Lord *literally* endures forever. The God who annihilates, however, does not everlastingly love or forgive.

Classic Universalism

The second afterlife view I reject says God places everyone in heaven. I call this view "classic universalism," and it says God single-handedly guarantees heavenly happiness for all.

Some biblical passages seem to support universalism. "As in Adam all die, so also in Christ shall all be made alive," says Paul.[5] We might interpret this passage to mean everyone enjoys life everlasting. God will "reconcile all things to himself," Paul argues elsewhere.[6] "No one is cast off by the Lord forever," says Lamentations, because God "will show compassion, so great is his unfailing love" (3:31-33).

Perhaps the most persuasive argument for universalism is general: a loving God forgives… everyone. "I blot out your transgressions," says God in the book of Isaiah, "and remember your sins no more" (43:25-26). Our "sins are forgiven," says John, for the sake of God's name (1 John 2:12).

Classic universalism assumes God has the power to ensure heaven for all. A sovereign God single-handedly secures bliss for all, despite what they've done or even want. Some universalists say this controlling is somehow compatible with creatures having freedom to reject God (e.g., Karl Barth). Others say God initially created us in such a way we'd eventually choose heaven (e.g., David Bentley Hart). These explanations sound like we're simultaneously free and pre-programmed, which makes no sense to me.

I like that classic universalism emphasizes God's love and forgiveness. I like that it says God sends no one to hell. But I don't like

---

5. 1 Cor. 15:22

6. Col. 1:20

what it assumes about God's power and creaturely freedom. And this view stands at odds with uncontrolling love. Let me explain.

First, a God with the power to put everyone in heaven single-handedly should use that power to stop evil now. And yet evil occurs. If God controls in the afterlife to ensure happiness, God ought to ensure happiness in the present. Or at least prevent horrific evils. In short, if God has controlling power, the world ought to be a much better place.

Second, the classic form of universalism ignores the freedom of those who *don't* want a loving relationship with God. It says, "You have to be in heaven, even if you don't want to be." The Apostle Paul says love does not force its own way (1 Cor. 13:5), but this view disagrees.

Third, if we all end up enjoying everlasting bliss no matter what we do, our actions don't *ultimately* matter. Our choices today don't really count if God single-handedly rescues us later. What we do is meaningless from an ultimate perspective.

Fourth, believing God sends everyone to eternal bliss undermines incentives to avoid evil, fight corruption, or combat climate change. Why self-sacrifice if it doesn't matter for eternity? It's hard to care about the present if God places everyone in eternal bliss.

Uncontrolling Love

All the afterlife theories we've explored—from Hamilton's view of hell to annihilation to classic universalism—say God can single-handedly decide our destinies. We're passive pawns. Each also faces an insurmountable problem: it's impossible to reconcile creaturely freedom with a God who controls creatures. The usual afterlife theories assume God alone does or could decide our future.

The relentless love view rejects the idea God does or even can control others. God's love is *inherently* uncontrolling. By "uncontrolling," I mean God cannot single-handedly determine any agent, circumstance, or outcome. Because God always loves everyone and everything, and because God's love can't control anyone or anything, God cannot singly determine what happens now or after death.

By "love," I mean God acts intentionally, in relational response, to promote overall well-being.[7] The Bible offers powerful reasons to think God loves all. This means God wants the well-being of all, not wanting any to perish (2 Pet. 3:9). God loves by promoting flourishing rather than condemning anyone to destruction, torture, or death.

The uncontrolling love view solves several problems. Perhaps the most important is the problem of evil. We all know that awful things happen, and there's unnecessary suffering in the world. If able, a truly loving God would prevent genuine evil. And yet evils persist.

The uncontrolling love view solves this problem and others by saying God simply can't prevent evil single-handedly. God *can't*. Consequently, we should not blame the God unable to control those who do evil.[8] God does empathize with sufferers, work to heal, try to squeeze good from bad, and call creatures to cooperate in God's work to overcome evil with good.[9]

With this basic explanation of uncontrolling love, let's turn to relentless love.

Relentless Love

The relentless love view starts from the truth of uncontrolling love. It says we have genuine but limited freedom, and because of

---

7. I explain this definition in detail in several books. See especially *Pluriform Love: An Open and Relational Theology of Well-Being* (Grasmere, ID: SacraSage, 2022).

8. For detailed explanations of my solution to the problem of evil, see *God Can't: How to Believe in God and Love after Tragedy, Abuse, and Other Evils* (Grasmere, ID: SacraSage, 2019); *The Uncontrolling Love of God: An Open and Relational Account of Providence* (Downers Grove, IL: IVP Academic, 2015); and *Pluriform Love*, chs. 6-7.

9. For details on these, see *God Can't*. For an answer to why evil is even possible if God is Creator, see *Pluriform Love*, ch. 7.

freedom, our choices truly matter. Relentless love also embraces the commonsense view that love is relational. Given these assumptions, this afterlife theory says God *needs* our cooperation for love to flourish… in this life and the next.

At the heart of relentless love is the idea God continues to love everlastingly beyond our bodily deaths. It builds from oft-repeated lines in the Psalms: "the steadfast love of God endures forever." The writer of Lamentations puts it this way: "The steadfast love of the Lord never ceases; his mercies never end." The relentless love view takes as straightforwardly true what the Apostle Paul writes in his love chapter: "Love never gives up; it always hopes; it always endures" (1 Cor. 13:7).

Other views of the afterlife assume God freely set up whatever rules God wanted, and God can keep or break them. These rules lead God single-handedly to determine the fate of everyone, whether this be heaven, hell, or annihilation. By contrast, relentless love says the ultimate rules derive from God's nature of love, which even God cannot change. Consequently, God necessarily loves everyone here and in the hereafter, and God forces no one to hell, heaven, or nothingness.

The relentless love view, therefore, disagrees with afterlife theories that say God *alone* decides our fate. We also play a role. When we cooperate with divine love, we enjoy well-being, goodness, and abundant life. Cooperating with love brings *shalom* and healing.

When we don't cooperate with God, the Lover of the Universe does not punish. But we suffer the natural negative consequences that come from failing to cooperate with love. These consequences are the "destruction" Paul talks about in Romans 9:22-24. Natural negative consequences accompany our saying no to positive and healthy choices, whether in this life or the next. To put it another way, sin is its own punishment.

Relentless love extends the logic of uncontrolling love everlastingly: God never quits on anyone. God's patience never ends.

Relentless Love Guarantees

The relentless love view does not guarantee everyone enjoys eternal bliss. An uncontrolling God cannot single-handedly ensure every creature cooperates, because cooperation is a free choice. But love is like that: it does not force its way (1 Cor. 13:5).

The relentless love view guarantees that love wins in other ways.[10]

First, the God whose nature is uncontrolling love *never* stops loving us. Because love comes first in God's nature, God *can't* stop loving. Many theologies say God may love us but could torture or destroy instead. I can't imagine a loving person sending people to everlasting hell or annihilating them. The God of relentless love, by contrast, *always* loves. Love wins, because it's guaranteed the God's relentless love always works for well-being.

Second, the relentless love view says those who say "Yes" to God's love in the afterlife experience heavenly happiness. Those who cooperate with love are guaranteed life eternal; they enjoy abundant life. Love wins, because it's guaranteed those who cooperate with God's relentless love enjoy afterlife bliss.

Third, God *never* stops inviting us to love and God doesn't punish. Although some may not cooperate in a particular moment, God never throws in the towel. The natural negative consequences are self-imposed, not divinely inflicted. Love wins, therefore, because it's guaranteed God always offers us the choice of love and never resorts to retribution.

Fourth, the relentless love view says the habits of love shape us into loving people. As we consistently say "Yes" to God in this life and the next, we develop loving characters. Those who consistently respond positively grow less and less likely to choose unloving options. Developing a loving character may happen quickly or take more time, but we become radically new creations as we cooperate

---

10. On the theme of love winning at the end, see Rob Bell, *Love Wins: A Book About Heaven, Hell, and the Fate of Every Person Who Ever Lived* (San Francisco: HarperCollins, 2011).

with our Creator. Love wins, because consistent cooperation with God's relentless love guarantees we develop loving characters.

Finally, we have good reason to *hope* all creatures will eventually cooperate with this patient God of love. It's reasonable to think the God whose patience is unlimited and whose love is universal will eventually convince everyone. But universal salvation cannot come through coercion. We have genuine hope all will eventually cooperate, because time is on the side of an everlastingly persuasive God.

Conclusion

God's loving patience gives witness to divine glory. Rather than lose patience and send some to hell, the glory of God's relentless love is manifest because God condemns no one to everlasting punishment. Rather than lose patience and annihilate some, the glory of God's relentless love is manifest because God never gives up inviting everyone to love. Rather than lose patience and force some to heaven by overriding their freedom, the glory of God's relentless love is manifest in God's patience to persuade rather than control.

The glory of God is manifest in patient yet relentless love!

CHAPTER 9

Reimagining God in the Old Testament

Eric A. Seibert

You might wonder what a chapter dealing with God in the Old Testament is doing in a book designed to deconstruct hell.[1] The Old Testament makes no mention of hell. Nor does it conceive of a two-storied afterlife in which sinners and saints are separated. Instead, the Old Testament refers to a place called Sheol, a shadowy underworld abode which receives all who die, righteous and unrighteous alike.[2] So how do people who believe in hell find support for this doctrine in the pages of the Old Testament? They do so by focusing on some of its most violent portrayals of God.

Linking God's Violent Old Testament Behavior to Eternal Suffering

Some Christians believe that God's fierce acts of divine judgment in the Old Testament anticipate God's wrath upon sinful humanity at the end of time. Just as God punished sinners in the Old Testament through warfare, natural disasters, plagues, and death,

---

1. Portions of this chapter are adapted from Eric A. Seibert, *Disturbing Divine Behavior: Troubling Old Testament Images of God* (Minneapolis: Fortress, 2009). Used by permission.
2. See, e.g., Gen.37:35; Num. 16:30-33; Ps. 89:48. Cf. Eccles. 9:1-3.

they reason, so God will punish sinners in the hereafter with eternal suffering. In this way, God's violent behavior toward the wicked in the Old Testament is thought to foreshadow, or prefigure, what God will do to the wicked at the consummation.

Numerous Old Testament scholars explicitly make this connection. According to Tremper Longman:

> The wars of the Old Testament and the end-time judgment are acts of divine judgment against evil. Indeed, we are to think that Joshua's battles are *a preview and a warning of the final judgment*.[3]

Similarly, Christopher Wright claims:

> The conquest of Canaan stands in Scripture as one of those signal events that points to the final judgment (along with other catastrophes like the flood, Sodom and Gomorrah, the fall of Babylon, etc.).[4]

Even some New Testament writers viewed certain Old Testament stories this way. As Wright observes:

> Some of the horror stories [in the Old Testament]…are recalled as examples and warnings: the flood (Matt. 24:36-41; 2 Peter 3:3-7); Sodom and Gomorrah (Matt. 10:15, 11:23-24); Korah (Jude 11); the wilderness plagues (1 Cor. 10:6-10), and even the conquest itself (Heb. 11:31). In all these cases, the historical, earthly judgments of God in the

---

3. Tremper Longman III, *Confronting Old Testament Controversies: Pressing Questions about Evolution, Sexuality, History, and Violence* (Grand Rapids: Baker, 2019), 199, emphasis mine. Longman (p. 200) builds on an idea Meredith Kline referred to as "Intrusion ethics." See Meredith G. Kline, *The Structure of Biblical Authority*, 2nd ed. (Eugene, OR: Wipf and Stock, 1997), 154-171.

4. Christopher J. H. Wright, *The God I Don't Understand: Reflections on Tough Questions of Faith* (Grand Rapids, MI: Zondervan, 2008), 96.

Old Testament are used as case studies and warnings in relation to the even worse judgment to come.[5]

For some, this linkage between God's violent behavior in the Old Testament and eschatological violence in the New Testament makes the doctrine of hell more reasonable.[6] As theologian Sharon Putt makes this observation when she writes, "Some of this acceptance of hell and of the violence it perpetuates eternally on the unfortunate sinners who dwell there comes from our interpretation of divine violence in the Bible."[7]

Severing the Link

If Putt is correct—and I believe she is—it behooves us to think very carefully about the way we interpret divine violence in Scripture, *especially* in the Old Testament. Do these violent portrayals of God reflect God's true nature and character? Do they reveal how God, the living God, actually behaved in time and space? If so, then perhaps the linkage between God's violent behavior in the Old Testament and the doctrine of eternal suffering is warranted. But if this is not what God is like, it is imperative to acknowledge this in order to sever this artificial link between God's alleged violence in the past and God's presumed violent behavior in the future.

In this chapter, I argue that violent portrayals of God in the Old Testament do *not* accurately reflect what God, the living God, is actually like. After making a few remarks about the ubiquity of divine violence in the Old Testament, and considering various ways scholars have attempted to justify God's violent behavior, I will suggest an alternative approach that deconstructs rather than defends divine violence in the Old Testament. Doing so demonstrates

---

5. Wright, *God I Don't Understand*, 81.

6. It is still extremely problematic since comparing temporal punishment to *eternal* suffering is wildly disproportionate.

7. Sharon L. Baker, *Razing Hell: Rethinking Everything You've Been Taught about God's Wrath and Judgment* (Louisville: Westminster John Knox, 2010), 52.

the fallacy of appealing to God's violence in the Old Testament to support the doctrine of hell.

Divine Violence in the Old Testament

There is a lot of violent behavior associated with God in the pages of the Old Testament. According to Professor Raymund Schwager, roughly one thousand Old Testament passages emphasize God's anger, violence, and vengeance, and more than one hundred additional passages contain God's commands to kill others.[8] In these 1,100 passages, God drowns humanity, sends plagues, hardens hearts, annihilates "sinners," instigates wars, and even commands genocide. By the time you reach the end of the Old Testament, God has killed (or sanctioned the killing of) nearly 2.5 million people.[9]

Obviously, all this death and destruction—ostensibly from the hand of God—bothers many readers, particularly Christian readers. Christians believe God to be loving, compassionate, patient, and kind. But how can such an exalted view of God be maintained in the presence of so much carnage?

Defending God's Violent Behavior in the Old Testament

Many interpreters rush to God's defense, strenuously trying to justify God's violent behavior in the Old Testament.[10] Though

---

8. Raymund Schwager, *Must There Be Scapegoats: Violence and Redemption in the Bible*, trans. Maria L. Assad (New York: Crossroad, 2000), 55, 60.

9. This is according to Steve Wells, *Drunk with Blood: God's Killings in the Bible* (USA: Giordano Press, 2010), 3. That number only includes casualties reported in the text. Wells (pp. 4-5) estimates the total would be approximately ten times higher if you were to include those killed in stories without body counts (the flood narrative, the destruction of Sodom and Gomorrah, etc.).

10. See, e.g., Paul Copan, *Is God a Moral Monster? Making Sense of the Old Testament God* (Grand Rapids, MI: Baker, 2011), and *Is God a Vindictive Bully? Reconciling Portrayals of God in the Old and New Testaments* (Grand Rapids, MI: Baker, 2022). Christopher J. H. Wright, *The God I Don't Understand: Reflections on Tough Questions of Faith* (Grand Rapids, MI: Zondervan, 2008), 86-108; David T. Lamb, *God Behaving Badly: Is the God of the Old Testament Angry, Sexist, and Racist?* (Downers Grove, IL: InterVarsity, 2011), 93-113; Tremper Longman III, *Confronting Old Testament Controversies: Pressing Questions about*

space doesn't allow for an extensive discussion of their efforts, a few comments will suffice to demonstrate the various ways these individuals attempt to exonerate God.

Some claim God was justified in killing people as punishment for their sin. We should not be surprised that God kills people, they say, since we are all sinners who deserve death (a very dubious theological claim, in my opinion). What should surprise us, they say, is that God allows any of us to live! Thus, when God orders Israelites to kill "wicked" Canaanites or annihilate "evil" Amalekites, these people are simply getting what they deserve (Deut. 9:4-5; 1 Sam. 15:2-3).

Others defend God's behavior by appealing to a greater good. God needed to wipe out Canaanites, for example, so that Israel's religious purity would not be comprised (Deut. 20:18). Keeping Israel pure was important because the Messiah would come through Israel, and it was the Messiah who would save the world. It's hard to imagine a "greater good" than that.

Still others appeal to mystery, claiming God's ways are higher than ours (Isa.55:9). As finite beings, we can't see the big picture. We don't know the whole story. We just have to trust that whatever God does is good and right because God is the one doing it.

Interpreters use approaches like these (and others) to free God from charges of wrongdoing. Though their arguments are made with more nuance and elaboration than I have space to explore here, I find them unsatisfying and ultimately unpersuasive.[11] Even if you believe some violent Old Testament stories might not be as bad as they first appear (e.g., numerous passages suggest not *all* Canaanites were killed), God is still responsible for an enormous

---

Evolution, Sexuality, History, and Violence (Grand Rapids, MI: Baker, 2019), 123-206; Dan Kimball, *How (Not) to Read the Bible: Making Sense of the Anti-Women, Anti-Science, Pro-Violence, Pro-Slavery and Other Crazy-Sounding Parts of Scripture* (Grand Rapids, MI: Zondervan, 2020), 253-91.

11. For a more extensive look at these approaches and my critique of them, see Seibert, *Disturbing Divine Behavior*, 69-88. See also Gregory A. Boyd, *Crucifixion of the Warrior God: Interpreting the Old Testament's Violent Portraits of God in Light of the Cross* (Minneapolis: Fortress, 2017), 1:379-414.

amount of bloodshed, killing, and harm in the pages of the Old Testament. It is difficult to see how these actions are consistent with the behavior of a good, loving, and morally perfect deity.

Deconstructing God's Violent Behavior in the Old Testament

Rather than tying ourselves in knots trying to explain why it was necessary for God to kill *every* firstborn Egyptian (Exod. 12:29-30) or to command Saul to massacre *all* Amalekite babies (1 Sam. 15:3), we should acknowledge that God, the living God, never sanctioned or participated in such violent acts. God did not say and do everything the Old Testament claims.[12] While culturally conditioned portrayals like these reflect how ancient Israelites conceived of God, they do not represent God's true nature and character.

So then how do we go about deconstructing these violent views of God? Allow me to suggest three interpretive strategies that can help in this endeavor.

Distinguish between the textual and actual God

First, when we read passages in the Bible that speak of God, it is crucial to distinguish "between the textual God and the actual God," to borrow language from Terence Fretheim.[13] The textual God is just that, words on a page, whereas the actual God is the living Word. Or to put it another way, the textual God is a literary representation (or a series of literary representations) in the Bible, whereas the actual God is a living reality, the one to whom our worship is directed.

The need to make distinctions between the textual and actual God is built into the very fabric of Scripture itself. It is clear that

---

12. For an extensive discussion of this claim, see Seibert, *Disturbing Divine Behavior*, 91-181.

13. Terence E. Fretheim and Karlfried Froehlich, *The Bible as Word of God: In a Postmodern Age* (Minneapolis: Fortress Press, 1998), 116.

some portrayals of God stand in stark contrast with others. For example, one passage claims God punishes "children for the iniquity of parents" while another emphatically states children will "*not* suffer for the iniquity of a parent" (Exod. 20:5; Ezek. 18:20, emphasis added).[14] One passage declares God to be "merciful and gracious," while another says God hardens people's hearts for the express purpose of allowing them to be slaughtered *without* mercy (Exod. 34:6; Josh.11:20). Competing and contrasting views of God are canonized in the pages of the Old Testament.

This contrast becomes even more striking when images of God in the Old Testament are compared to images of God in the New Testament. Unless we are willing to concede that God's character is utterly inconsistent, these diverse representations of God cannot all be accurate. They force us to make choices about what God is really like. Sometimes the Bible reveals God's character; other times it distorts it.[15] Violent Old Testament portrayals of God are one of those distortions.

It is not surprising that Israel portrayed God this way. Their neighbors did the same. The violent nature of the gods was a theological given in antiquity, unquestioned and embraced by people everywhere. For instance, people in the ancient world believed that gods engaged in warfare and were ultimately responsible for victory and defeat in battle. This is easily demonstrated with numerous texts and inscriptions.[16] Since Israel was part and parcel of that environment, it is natural to find them conceiving of God in similar ways. Thus, rather than revealing something unique about God's character, these violent Old Testament portrayals simply reflect the historical milieu of which they were a part. In short, they say more

---

14. All Scripture references are taken from the New Revised Standard Version (NRSV) of the Bible.

15. This language of revealing and distorting God's character is from Jack Nelson-Pallmeyer, *Jesus Against Christianity: Reclaiming the Missing Jesus* (Harrisburg, PA: Trinity, 2001). See, e.g., pp. 16, 65, 88, 137.

16. For examples, see Sa-Moon Kang, *Divine War in the Old Testament and in the Ancient Near East* (New York: de Gruyter, 1989).

about the cultural context from which they emerged than they do about the true nature of God.

Since violent portrayals of God distort God's character, they should be recognized for what they are: culturally conditioned representations of God. While it is true that these depictions do reflect *Israel's* beliefs about God, they do *not* reflect God's true character.

Follow Jesus' Lead in Rejecting Violent Old Testament Portrayals of God

We can also deconstruct violent views of God by following Jesus' lead. Jesus was very selective about which Old Testament images he endorsed and which images he did not. Jesus embraced and promoted Old Testament views of God that reflected God's love, compassion, and mercy, while largely ignoring those which portray God's wrath, violence, and retribution.[17] Apparently, Jesus believed some Old Testament views of God were serviceable while others were not.

We witness this at the very beginning of Jesus' ministry. In his hometown synagogue in Nazareth, Jesus takes the scroll of Isaiah and reads:

> The Spirit of the Lord is upon me, because he has anointed me to bring good news to the poor. He has sent me to proclaim release to the captives and recovery of sight to the blind, to let the oppressed go free, to proclaim the year of the Lord's favor (Luke 4:18-19).

What is striking about this reading is the simple fact that Jesus stops mid-sentence. The verse goes on to speak about "the day of vengeance of our God" (Isa. 61:2). But Jesus stops just prior

---

17. For a discussion of passages in the Gospels concerning eschatological judgment along with those thought to suggest Jesus believed the coming destruction of Jerusalem would be an act of divine judgment, see Seibert, *Disturbing Divine Behavior*, 243-261.

"to the prophetic punch line."[18] The part Jesus omits refers to the much-anticipated day of the Lord when Israel believed God would intervene to punish their enemies.[19]

The Old Testament routinely portrays God as being hostile toward the wicked and those who do evil. In Psalm 3:7 the Psalmist says God "break(s) the teeth of the wicked," and in Psalm 145:20 the Psalmist claims that the Lord "will destroy" the wicked. But Jesus suggests precisely the opposite. In the Sermon on the Mount, Jesus describes God as one who "is kind to the ungrateful and wicked" (Luke 6:35). Apparently, Jesus had a rather different view of God's attitude toward the wicked than many Old Testament passages suggest.

This is also evident by the way Jesus challenged violent views of God rooted in Israel's beliefs about divine reward and punishment. Despite the Old Testament's insistence that God punishes sinners and rewards the righteous,[20] Jesus seems to understand God's character quite differently. Jesus claims God extends goodness to everyone regardless of how they behave. According to Jesus, God "makes his sun rise on the evil and on the good, and sends rain on the righteous and on the unrighteous" (Matt 5:45). In other words, God gives good gifts to everyone indiscriminately. God is not nice to the righteous and mean to the wicked. God is kind to all. God's gracious provisions are lavished upon everyone, however worthy or unworthy they may be.[21]

Some of Jesus' parables also demonstrate a different vision of God then violent Old Testament portrayals suggest. While it is true

18. C. S. Cowles, "The Case for Radical Discontinuity," in *Show Them No Mercy: Four Views on God and Canaanite Genocide*, C. S. Cowles, et al. (Grand Rapids, MI: Zondervan, 2003), 24.

19. For a discussion of potential ways to understand the meaning of this omission, see Richard B. Hays, *Echoes of Scripture in the Gospels* (Waco, TX: Baylor University Press, 2016), 226-228.

20. See Deuteronomy 28 for an extensive example.

21. Some material in this paragraph is adapted from Eric A. Seibert, *Disarming the Church: Why Christians Must Forsake Violence to Follow Jesus and Change the World* (Eugene, OR: Cascade, 2018), 69.

that God pursues sinners, Jesus makes it clear that God does so to save them, not slaughter them. The three parables of the lost sheep, the lost coin, and the lost (prodigal) son in Luke 15 make this point exquisitely.

While Jesus clearly builds his view of God from the Old Testament, as his strategic use of two Old Testament stories in Luke 4 illustrates,[22] Jesus feels no compulsion to uncritically accept every portrayal he finds there. Rather, he uses Old Testament images of God selectively, affirming some, while distancing himself from others. In this way, Jesus demonstrates deep respect for the "Old Testament" without perpetuating some of its most problematic views of God.[23] We should do likewise.

Believe in a God of Love

Finally, we can deconstruct violent views of God by recognizing the implications of our affirmation that "God is love" (1 John 4:16). As theologian Tom Oord observes in his recent book, *Open and Relational Theology*:

> God's unchanging nature is love....love is what God does.... love comes logically first among divine attributes....God cannot *not* love.[24]

Everything we know about who God is and what God does must be consistent with the nature of love. "Open and relational

---

22. Jesus cites two Old Testament narratives, one about a Sidonian widow (1 Kings 17:8-16), the other about a Syrian general (2 Kings 5:1-14). Each story describes divine assistance to a foreigner, thereby emphasizing the inclusive nature of God's care and compassion.

23. *Contra* Longman who claims "there is no conflict between Jesus and the God of the Old Testament" and "that Jesus himself fully embraced the Old Testament without qualification" (*Confronting Old Testament Controversies*, 162).

24. Thomas Jay Oord, *Open and Relational Theology: An Introduction to Life-Changing Ideas* (Grasmere, ID: SacraSage, 2021), 124, emphasis original.

theology uses the logic of love to make sense of what God can and can't do."[25]

Violence is antithetical to love. Love looks out for the interests of others, while violence promotes the interests of the perpetrator. Love serves, yet violence dominates. Love is uncontrolling and self-giving.[26] Violence exercises "power over" and takes what it wants by force.[27]

Tom Oord defines love this way: "To love is to act intentionally, in relational response to God and others, to promote overall well-being."[28] The final part of this definition, the idea that love promotes overall well-being, is especially helpful for our purposes. If God *is* love, that means God is always working to promote the well-being of all life.

Yet this is utterly inconsistent with God's violent behavior in the Old Testament. How does commanding the annihilation of Amalekites promote the overall well-being of the women and men, soldiers and civilians, toddlers and infants who were slaughtered (1 Sam. 15:3)? Or how does giving one man's wives to another so they can be raped in public view promote the overall well-being of the women being sexually assaulted (2 Sam. 12:11)? And how can it be loving to order a woman to return and submit to an abuser (Gen.16:1-9), or to strike an innocent child with a terminal illness (2 Sam. 12:13-19), or to send lions to kill people who don't worship the Lord (2 Kings 17:25)? Yet the Old Testament claims God does all these things and *many* more. Rather than promoting overall well-being, God's violent behavior in the Old Testament does considerable harm.

---

25. Oord, *Open and Relational Theology*, 78.

26. This language comes from Thomas Jay Oord, *The Uncontrolling Love of God: An Open and Relational Account of Providence* (Downers Grove, IL: InterVarsity, 2015), 151-86.

27. Gregory A. Boyd, *The Myth of a Christian Nation: How the Quest for Political Power is Destroying the Church* (Grand Rapids, MI: Zondervan, 2005), 18. Boyd uses the language of "power over" to describe "the kingdom of the world."

28. Thomas Jay Oord, *Pluriform Love: An Open and Relational Theology of Well-Being* (Grasmere, ID: SacraSage, 2022), 28.

Whatever we believe about God must be consistent with our understanding of love. Affirming that God is love—and working out the implications of that affirmation—enables us to deconstruct violent views of God in the pages of the Old Testament. Since violence (which involves doing harm to others) and love (which involves promoting the well-being of others) are mutually exclusive, it stands to reason that a loving God cannot be a violent God.

Conclusion

Rather than defending God's violent behavior in the Old Testament, we should be deconstructing it. This is accomplished by distinguishing between the textual and actual God, following Jesus in selectively using Old Testament portrayals of God, and affirming that God is love. Because God is love, and love does no harm, we can say with confidence that God, the living God, has *never* engaged in acts of violence, Old Testament portrayals notwithstanding.

Deconstructing these violent views of God effectively severs the link that has been forged between divine violence in the Old Testament and final judgment in the New Testament. This removes one of the supporting arguments for the dreadful doctrine of hell so many Christians have mistakenly accepted. Deconstructing violent views of God also allows us to see God more clearly, enabling us to reimagine God in ways that are congruent with the God revealed in Jesus, a God of love, compassion, and grace. Hopefully, this will encourage people to enter more deeply into a relationship with God, the actual God, the one who loves lavishly and invites us to do the same.

CHAPTER 10

Inescapably Ingrained: How Western Culture Perpetuates the Everlasting Torment View of Hell

Shawn M. Ryan

"People think it's the flames that make Hell unbearable. It's not. It is the absence of love."[1] —The Reverend (Guy Pearce)

Introduction

In the brutal and violent 2016 movie, *Brimstone*, the Reverend is not the good guy. But his comment holds value in both what people think and what may be reality. Belief in an afterlife of eternal suffering and torment has been ingrained in modern Christianity. But it is not simply Christians who hold on to this view. It permeates Western culture. It's seen in the above quote, but it is also found in countless other mediums. In our capitalistic society, the idea of a fiery place of suffering sells, and it sells well. Musical artists

---

1. *Brimstone*, directed by Martin Koolhoven (N279 Entertainment, 2016), accessed April 24, 2022, https://tubitv.com.

and rock bands have used the fiery pits of hell as a visual and lyrical medium for decades. Artists such as Black Sabbath, AC/DC, and Lamb of God, have found immense success in terms of fandom and financial gain by playing on the idea of eternal suffering. (This is not a judgment of these artists; in fact, they may believe their musings to be true. They, too, are part of the culture with this vision of hell.) It is even seen in animated shows. The Simpsons had an episode in its fourth season where Homer says to God, "I'm not a bad guy. I work hard and I love my kids. So why should I spend half of my Sunday hearing about how I'm going to Hell?[2] The visual representation of an angel and devil on the shoulder has been found in numerous cartoons and animated movies, from The Simpsons to The Flintstones, to Disney movies and shorts, to Tom & Jerry, and more. The red, horned, pitchfork-wielding devil whispering in the ear of a character is pervasive.

Clearly, the view of eternal suffering has far-reaching exposure through many types of media. With so much found in animation, not to mention church teachings, it is not surprising that people grow up with these ideas embedded in their psyche. This is made more evident when Pew Research shows that even a small percentage of atheists and agnostics believe in the existence of hell. In 2014, Pew found that three percent of atheists, nine percent of agnostics, and thirty-six percent of the "nothing-in-particular" group all believe in hell, including twenty-two percent that say religion is not important.[3] These are groups of non-religious people, who question or deny the existence of a deity, yet they believe in hell! Another Pew Research study completed in 2021, showed that sixty-two percent (which is up from fifty-eight percent in 2014) of all U.S. adults believe in the existence of hell, with Evangelical

2. *The Simpsons*, season 4, episode 3, "Homer the Heretic," directed by Jim Reardon, aired October 8, 1992, on FOX, accessed April 24, 2022, https://www.disneyplus.com.

3. Caryle Murphy, "Most Americans believe in heaven and hell," Pew Research Center, November 10, 2015, accessed April 24, 2022, https://www.pewsearch.org/fact-tank/2015/11/10/most-americans-believe-in-heaven-and-hell/.

Christians having the highest percentage at ninety-one percent.[4] Belief in hell flows across the Western world, making it not only a religious perspective but a cultural one.

The purpose of this essay is not to argue the merits of this belief. There are a considerable number of other sources with that as their intention. My current aim is to focus on how affirming a hell that entails eternal torment is ingrained in Western culture and how this fact may be detrimental to multiple facets of Christian practice.

The Core Principle (Love)

The biblical text undoubtedly presents depictions that many use to justify belief in eternal suffering. The concept was not simply made up without any foundational support from the sacred scriptures. Unfortunately, those that point to certain stories, or use prooftexts, to make the argument for eternal suffering seem to neglect the merciful, non-judgmental, unconditional love of the triune god. This essay does not opine on the inerrancy or infallibility of scripture, but it does take into consideration the overarching themes found from Genesis to Revelation and throughout the Apocrypha. It stands on the principle of what John wrote, which is that "God is love."[5] All views and beliefs must be filtered through that fundamental truth; love is the essential characteristic of the creator. Paul is bold about the deep love God has for us when he says:

---

4. "Views on the afterlife: Majorities of U.S. adults say they believe in heaven, hell," Pew Research Center, November 23, 2021, accessed April 24, 2022, https://www.pewrearch. org/religion/2021/11/23/views-on-the-afterlife/. Added details show that in every group classification a higher percentage of people believe in Heaven than Hell, and this holds true for all Christian groups, Unaffiliated groups, age groups, and even political and geographical groups. A similar survey completed by the Barna Group also had a high percentage of those believing in Hell, but the details break it down into more categories of what Hell may actually be.

5. 1 John 4:8 (NASB).

*"Who will separate us from the love of Christ? Will tribula-
tion, or trouble, or persecution, or famine, or nakedness, or
danger, or sword? Just as it is written, 'For your sake we are
killed all day long; we are regarded as sheep to be slaughtered.'
But in all these things we overwhelmingly conquer through
him who loved us. For I am convinced that neither death,
nor life, nor angels, nor principalities, nor things present, nor
things to come, nor powers, nor height, nor depth, nor any
other thing created will be able to separate us from the love of
God that is in Christ Jesus our Lord."*[6]

Paul is known to have written some challenging and even some
confrontational things throughout all his epistles[7], but here he is
in line with John on the importance of love and the role it plays in
our relationship with God.

Hard to Break the Cycle

So how is possible that we have a cultural view of hell which stands
contrary to the biblical depiction of a loving god? Let us use an
analogy to supply a partial answer.

Pretend there is a person isolated on a remote island from
birth and only a select few adults to guide and teach her about the
world. As a thought experiment, the child is taught that the sky
and ocean were green, and the grass and trees were blue. This is
all the child knows, and she believes it to be true. While growing
up, she naturally associates all variants of those colors as different
shades of what she was taught. When the child becomes an adult,
she moves to a more populated part of the earth and hears someone

---

6. Romans 8:35-39 (NASB).

7. Since Paul is attributed to writing the majority of the NT, there are plenty of areas
where it seems he may have differed from other biblical writers on certain topics, or at
least he worded things differently enough that causes conflict for readers and has divided
otherwise devout people on some theological stances. There are also challenges to his
authorship of several books.

comment, "The sky is a beautiful shade of blue today hovering over that field of rolling green grass." Of course, this would be a shock to the now fully grown human! All that she ever knew was that the sky was green, and the grass was blue, and now the opposite is said like it is fact. At first, she might argue about the colors. But as others confirm reality, she faces a crisis, and fights hard against this new oppositional claim. Much is the same when someone hears a teaching that contradicts eternal suffering. It is hard to process, and even harder to move beyond what you have always known or thought to be true.

What's more, when a belief permeates throughout a culture, it affects people that claim to be counter-cultural. Those called into ministry are a great example. They too are exposed to depictions of damnation, of hell-fire and brimstone. So, when using scripture, they naturally seek out justification for those beliefs. Since the pastor, minister or priest has now solidified the belief in eternal torment as truth, she wants to teach it as such. This aids in the cycle that flows through the culture.

Of course, some members of the clergy do not talk openly about their views of hell. This may be due to their own questioning, or even because they do not want to lose congregants. But this tactic can backfire. When people are not taught opposing views or given the tools to investigate for themselves, they are left with nothing to stand on but the inherent cultural perspective. Being silent on the matter allows the cultural view to reign supreme. This is why it is important to actively oppose such misconceptions. It is vital to teach that which holds continuity with a god of love.

Consequences of Teaching Torment

Aside from the inaccurate depiction of a loving god, other consequences may be detrimental to a person's relationship with the divine. Far from being all-inclusive, I would like to give a few examples. First, for most Protestants, particularly Evangelicals, there is only one ingredient needed for people to find everlasting life: faith.

But how is the concept of faith alone compatible with the teaching of eternal suffering? To preach the avoidance of torment leads to a fear-based faith, which results in a works-based faith system. Teaching eternal suffering is teaching people to believe right, to act right, to worship right, or face everlasting torment and pain. This is not faith alone, as believers must take certain steps to avoid suffering. The end result may lead the congregant away from the church altogether, as she is being asked to do the impossible. Furthermore, it must be remembered that perfect love casts out fear.[8]

Another reason teaching hell as eternal suffering fails, is quite simply that it does not seem to work as a deterrent to negative behavior. Looking at the above Pew Research, the number of people in the United States that believe in hell is plainly counter-intuitive to the current prison population. In fact, the United States holds roughly twenty-five percent of the world's prison population, totaling about 2.19 million prisoners.[9] That is an enormous number of people. In a country with a high percentage of believers in hell, this seems puzzling. But that is only the case if teaching eternal suffering worked to deter people from sins and crimes. Intriguingly, what these numbers do affirm are the attitudes of justice, punishment, and vengeance in the United States. There is a clear guilty until proven innocent mindset held by the masses, and there is a quick judgment on another's behavior. This is an additional consequence of teaching eternal suffering; retributive punishment based on one's belief of another's actions.

A final consequence I will detail is the direct conflict that a belief in eternal conscious torment has with the Gospel, the good news of Jesus. This idea that one may believe in Christ but her friends and family that are loved could face eternal torment is not in line with good news at all. In fact, it's the exact opposite. Most

---

8. 1 John 4:18

9. *Prison Population by State 2022,* World Population Review, accessed May 31, 2022, https://worldpopulationreview.com/state-rankings/prison-population-by-state. It must be noted that there are cases of wrongful imprisonment and not all who face penalty are guilty. The point is not as much about the exceptions but the generalities.

people would find eternity to be quite hot and painful, which is not good news for anyone. Teaching torment greatly affects weekly sermons and other church gatherings. Many weekly messages serve to make people feel guilt and shame. They offer "good news" that they may be redeemed and spend eternity with Christ, but the focus tends to always be on the negative.

It is not just in the sermon messages, but also in songs of worship. Just take one popular song, "I Thank God", into consideration. Its lyrics have people singing they are weary souls, bags of bones, and drifting vagabonds. There is an interlude that tells them if Jesus saved me, he can do it for you, and a bridge with a line that says, "Hell lost another one, I am free."[10] Sermons and songs that guilt you into redemption are only good news when there is a fear of eternal suffering.

Finding a Better Way

What is good news, however, is that the depiction of hell as a place of everlasting torment isn't the only game in town. Earlier in this essay, I mentioned there were some biblical passages that could be used to support eternal suffering. However, one of the first reasons the reader who wants to stay loyal to the biblical witness should feel the freedom to oppose this view is that several other perspectives have biblical support. And some may argue they have more support. In 1997 Zondervan published a book titled *Four Views on Hell* that included arguments for the literal view, the metaphorical view, the purgatorial view, and the conditional view.[11] In 2016, a second edition with all new contributors was published which included some new considerations such as the universalist view.[12]

---

10. Maverick City Music & Upperroom, "I Thank God", track #7 on *Move Your Heart,* Maverick City Music, 2021.

11. Contributors to this edition included John F. Walvoord, William V. Crockett, Zachary J. Hayes, and Clark H. Pinnock. A revised edition was published in 2010.

12. This second edition had contributions from Denny Burk, John G. Stackhouse Jr., Robin A. Parry, and Jerry L. Walls.

There are clearly some aspects of overlap in the two publications, but they both show that eternal suffering is not the only viable choice.

In truth, the biblical witness portrays an unclear view of hell, which shows why opposition to the cultural view as the only acceptable one is paramount. To further understand the importance of the matter, consider the following quote by well-known and respected scholar N.T. Wright.

> *"My proposition is that the traditional picture of people going to either heaven or hell as a one-stage postmortem journey (with or without the option of some kind of purgatory or continuing journey as an intermediate stage) represents a serious distortion and diminution of the Christian hope."*[13]

Interestingly, it is not just scholars and theologians that recognize the ambiguity of scripture. In the classic novel *To Kill a Mockingbird*, Miss Maudie tells Scout that she may not understand, "but sometimes the Bible in the hand of one man is worse than a whiskey bottle in the hand of [another]... There are just some kind of men...who're so busy worrying about the next world they've never learned to live in this one..."[14] Fortunately, some pastors recognize this as well. In a recent sermon I attended at a local congregation, the pastor was talking about the Kingdom of God. He spoke of how it is not just some distant thought in the future, but how "It is in the here and now." He said, "But some pastors are so heavenly-minded they are earthly no good."[15] This statement exemplified to me that some clergy are so focused on a

---

13. N.T. Wright, *Surprised by Hope: Rethinking Heaven, the Resurrection, and the Mission of the Church* (New York: HarperOne, 2018), 148.

14. Harper Lee, *To Kill a Mockingbird* (New York: Harpers, 2006), 46.

15. Rev. Johnnie Blair, "The Parables of Jesus" (sermon, June 12, 2022). This is the lead pastor at my local church and the quote was used with his permission. I want to be clear that he was not talking about Hell specifically, but he was aware of the context of this essay to where the quote would be utilized.

future heaven they are not able to be present and not able to love people now. They are focused on leading people to a future wonderment when they could be living in the Kingdom of God today.

Another reason to oppose eternal suffering is that it helps one stay pragmatically consistent when trying to portray a relational, all-loving being, who wants us to love in return. If we stop condemning people to hell in our own minds, we can start to love everyone for who they are, and not where we judge they will spend eternity. We can change from a fear-based faith to one founded in love, from the god who is love. For those that adhere to an open and relational theological mindset, the god who is love is bad news for eternal suffering. In Exodus, it is taught that Pharaoh's heart was hardened. Some think the words, "But the Lord hardened Pharaoh's heart..."[16] was an action directed at Pharaoh by God. However, instead, it could be God's actions of love and wanting to free the Hebrews were so contrary to Pharaoh's heart that it became hardened. It was a consequence of who Pharaoh was, not a decree from God. God's love is appalling to some, and it is appalling because of their views of justice and punishment, and those views may lead to a hardening of the heart, they may lead to a strong belief in eternal suffering. But God wants to set his people free.

Most of what has been said thus far is with the mindset of teaching torment, but counseling has its place in culture as well. It's one thing to preach and teach varying views from the pulpit or in a small group setting, and another in a one-to-one counseling session. When I first started attending my church over ten years ago, I brought some questions to the pastor in direct personal communication. They were questions about God's love and hell.

I had asked these same questions to other pastors previously. However, this time the response was different. In the past, I had been answered in a manner implying my questions should not be asked. Or the Bible was just thrown in my face like it would answer all the issues I had raised. This time, instead of spouting verses or

---

16. Exodus 9:12 (NASB).

berating me about my concerns, this pastor simply said, "I don't know, those are tough questions." The non-answer was the best answer I ever received.

We kept talking and eventually got to the Bible and discovered some verses to consider while maintaining that the answers were not black and white, and the text retained its ambiguity. In this particular case, opposition to eternal suffering was not specifically taught, but the approach was how it should be in a counseling session. Recognize the person's concerns genuinely and truly try to understand. Admit the Bible leaves room for interpretation and then discuss some of those varying interpretations.

Unfortunately, many pastors, priests, and ministers look so much towards saving someone's soul from hell that they are not able to listen. Counseling is more personal than this, and if someone comes asking about hell, she should not be pushed into a fire simply for posing the question.

Conclusion

I want to conclude with a personal story about my early views of hell. I did not grow up in the church, only going on rare occasions with friends. My first thoughts about hell were solely culturally based (and they still may have been even if I grew up in church). This idea of eternal pain, torment, and suffering was at odds with other things I believed about the Christian god. My belief was that God was all-loving, and the only way to everlasting life was through his son Jesus. However, at the time, those beliefs caused a conflict for me that I could not reconcile. This all-loving deity was going to send most people that ever walked the face of the earth to hell; torment! pain! suffering! In my limited understanding, I thought that Christianity made up about one-quarter to one-third of the total current world population, which meant all others were bound for that horrid destination. It also meant that all those that lived before Christ were in a fiery pit burning endlessly. I held two opposing cultural views; God is love and those that do not believe are tortured, and I could not find reconciliation.

So, what was my alternative? I simply just did not believe. I became agnostic, and I lived as if I were an atheist. There was no daily thought about God or Christ. Instead, Christianity was just another system trying to provide understanding to the unknown. It was no different than other religions that currently thrived, or those that have died and only survive in historical sources.

Had someone taught me a different view, an oppositional view to eternal suffering, I would have found my way to accepting God, Jesus, and the Christian movement into my life much sooner. In a nutshell, teaching eternal suffering did not draw me into faith, but was a key catalyst in my lack of it!

CHAPTER 11

Engaging Cultures of Oppression

Meghan R. Henning

The past fifty years has seen a fierce debate about the ethics of eternal damnation and the nature of hell. In the aftermath of the violence of the twentieth century, many Christians worry about whether a good God can punish people for all eternity and whether hell is less fire and brimstone than solitude and the absence of God. This conversation has largely been had among white male scholars.

Whose Sin? Hell is Not an Equal Opportunity Punisher

What is forgotten in this badly needed conversation is that our theories of hell do not just describe punishment, they decide and prescribe culpability. Hell is not an equal opportunity punisher. In the early Christian apocalypses that describe hell graphic bodily tortures that "fit the crime" are tied to specific sins that were committed on earth. These punishments not only mirror ancient ideas about criminal justice, but the sins also mirror ancient ideas about gender, sex, and family.

In early Christian hell, young women bore the full burden of chastity, just as they would according to ancient Roman sexual norms. In his most famous sermon, Jesus preached that men should avoid hell by plucking out their eyes rather than looking lustfully upon a woman.[1] So it's pretty remarkable that later Christian hells see chastity as the purview of women and women alone.

The second century Apocalypse of Peter envisions young women who did not retain their virginity having their flesh torn apart by birds (the same punishment that the Greeks envisioned for the rape of Leto in Odyssey 11).[2] Their male paramours are nowhere to be seen. And in the Apocalypse of Paul, an early fifth century apocalypse that is otherwise very keen to punish male and female sinners right alongside each other, girls who had sex before marriage are punished alone, wearing black and shackled with fiery chains around their necks.[3]

While these sins and punishments don't jibe with the Sermon on the Mount, they do fit well with ancient Roman sexual norms in which a young woman's first sexual encounter was framed in terms of its economic value to her parents.[4] The Christian visions of hell intensified the ancient commodification of young women's bodies and assigned it theological significance—they, not their parents, will pay the price in hell, their bodies broken and enslaved, failing to achieve union with God.

Even though the Christian tours of hell punished both men and women for adultery, women were singled out as particularly responsible. In the Acts of Thomas a sex worker is murdered by her Christian lover who is angry that she will not marry him.[5] After

---

1. Matthew 5:27-30.

2. Apocalypse of Peter 11.

3. Apocalypse of Paul 39; the same punishment is also handed down in Ep. Tit. ll. 407–8; Lat. Vis. Ezra 43–44.

4. See Elizabeth A. Castelli, "Virginity and Its Meaning for Women's Sexuality in Early Christianity," *JFSR* 2 (1986), 61-88; on the representation of the Christian virgin in ascetic literature, see Teresa M. Shaw, "The Virgin Charioteer and the Bride of Christ: Gender and the Passion in Late Ancient Ethics and Early Christian Writings on Virginity," in *A Feminist Companion to Patristic Literature*, ed. Amy-Jill Levine and Maria Mayo Robbins, (T. & T. Clark, 2008) 193–210. On the material value of virginity in the medieval period, see Kim M. Phillips, "Four Virgins' Tales: Sex and Power in Medieval Law," in *Medieval Virginities*, eds. Anke Bernau, Ruth Evans, and Sarah Salih (Toronto: University of Toronto Press, 2003), 80–101.

5. Acts of Thomas 51-58.

her murder she tours hell and sees the punishments of women who commit adultery and sex workers, but male adulterers or murderers (like her male sexual partner) are noticeably absent.

The murdered sex worker who tours this hell is not being singled out simply because of her social status. Many of the earliest tours of hell place more of the blame on women, damning not just adultery, but anything a woman might do that attracts the attention of men in the first place. Women are punished in hell for their ornate hair styles, going out without a head covering, cosmetics, and even nursing in public places.[6] While in our world none of these things, least of all nursing one's child, would necessarily be a step on the road towards a sexual encounter, ancient sexual ethics sexualized every part of a woman's body and held her culpable for every stray hair and nip slip. These double standards in hell also reflect Roman sexual ethics in which the blame for adultery fell on the adulteress more than the adulterer, and a married man was only considered an adulterer if he had sex with a properly married woman.[7] In early Christian hell, women were damned for anything that compromised a household and societal order in which men were dominant.

What the history of hell also charts is the way in which women gradually became responsible for all familial sin including infant abandonment, and abortion. The earliest mentions of abortion hold men and women culpable for terminated pregnancies.[8] And in the earliest Christian tours of hell men and women are punished

---

6. Apocalypse of Peter 7, Acts of Thomas 56, Apocalypse of Paul 39, Latin Vision of Ezra 16-17, Chronicles of Jerahmeel 16.4.

7. Thomas McGinn, *Prostitution, Sexuality, and the Law in Ancient Rome* (New York: Oxford University Press, 1998), 147–56, argues that the Roman legal definition of adultery largely hinged upon the social status of the woman. If she was *matrona* or *mater familias*, then she and her partner were liable under the law. Women who were enslaved, prostitutes, procuresses, peregrines (foreign women not married to a Roman citizen), or convicted adulteresses were exempt from the law. As a result there were a lot of extramarital sexual relationships a married man could engage in that were not considered adulterous. Amy Richlin, "Approaches to the Sources on Adultery at Rome," *Women's Studies* 8 (1981): 225–50, 228.

8. *Didache* 2.2, *Epistle of Barnabas* 19.5.

for infanticide and infant exposure. The Apocalypse of Paul, one of the most widely read visions of hell, punishes both men and women who procure abortions to conceal adultery.[9] But in later medieval apocalypses like the Latin Vision of Ezra, women alone are responsible for becoming parents, and the men who procure abortions to conceal adultery are absent in hell, even though they were often the driving force behind this practice in antiquity.[10]

In the same way medieval women became responsible for the familial sins of others and could be punished for failing to breast-feed the off-spring of other families. The Greek Apocalypse of Ezra punishes women who "begrudge giving their breast" and the Latin Vision of Ezra punishes women who did not offer their breasts to infants and orphans.[11] Their punishments? They hang by their hair while beasts or snakes drink from their breasts.

Whose Torture? Whose Body? The Body Politics of Eternal Punishment

When we talk about hell today, it is not the "outer darkness where there is weeping and gnashing of teeth" of Matthew's gospel that people imagine. Rather, hell immediately calls up a fiery space with bodily tortures that "fit" the sin committed in some way. Why? In part, because the hell described in Dante's Inferno has left an indelible mark on our world.

The *Divine Comedy* has become a western literary classic, and continues to be read widely by Christians and non-Christians. As a result, many of Dante's depictions of hell, purgatory, and heaven are seared in our collective memory. Dante completed his *Divine Comedy*, just a year before his death, in 1320. Although it is a me-dieval text, the Inferno consciously reaches back to antiquity for its

---

9. Apocalypse of Paul 40.

10. Latin Vision of Ezra 52-53; Ovid, the Roman poet, for instance, had multiple adul-terous affairs that resulted in conception, but he criticized his mistresses harshly for hav-ing abortions (*Amores* 2.13).

11. Greek Apocalypse of Ezra 5.1-6; Latin Vision of Ezra 54.

vision of the afterlife. Dante sees the ancient Roman poet Virgil as his predecessor, modeling his own tour of hell in the *Inferno* after book six of Virgil's *Aeneid*, and even taking Virgil along on his trip. In spite of the prominent place of Virgil in his oeuvre, the graphic descriptions of punishments and their association with specific sins are modeled after the *Apocalypse of Paul*, an early Christian text that was very popular at the time when Dante wrote. The "measure for measure" punishments that are rooted in *lex talionis*, the ancient "law of retaliation," are foundational for Dante's vision of the afterlife.[12]

For Dante and his readers these lines of influence are part of what "authorizes" his vision, but they should give today's readers pause. The *Apocalypse of Paul* and other tours of hell like it took ancient Roman modes of torture and ideas about the body and gave them God's stamp of approval in an eternal system of justice. The punishments we find in early Christian hell are the punishments that Romans reserved for those of low social status: imprisonment in dark mines, hanging, beheading, being thrown to wild beasts, or burning alive.[13] The geography of ancient hell mirrors the context of one of antiquity's most degrading punishments, forced labor in underground mines.[14] In the mines prisoners rarely saw sunlight,

---

12. See Martha Himmelfarb, *Tours of Hell: An Apocalyptic Form in Jewish and Christian Literature* (Philadelphia: University of Pennsylvania Press, 1983), 68–105, for a summary of the various kinds of measure-for-measure punishments that occur in the apocalyptic tours of hell. See also Patrick Gray, "Abortion, Infanticide, and the Social Rhetoric of the Apocalypse of Peter," *JECS* 9 (2001): 313–37; Callie Callon, "Sorcery, Wheels, and Mirror Punishment in the Apocalypse of Peter," *JECS* 18, no. 1 (2010): 29–49; István Czachesz, "Torture in Hell and Reality: The Visio Pauli," in *The Visio Pauli and the Gnostic Apocalypse of Paul*, eds. Jan N. Bremmer and István Czachesz (Leuven: Peeters, 2007), 130–43. On judicial punishment as retribution for a crime in the Roman world, see Julia Hillner, *Prison, Punishment and Penance in Late Antiquity* (Cambridge: Cambridge University Press, 2015), 26, 36, 49, 50, 54, 62, 71, 96.

13. Smoke, heat, and damp were common forms of torture, along with the rack, the wheel, and the whip.

Hillner, *Prison, Punishment and Penance*, 51, 242–78, 339; Hillner argues, "The idea that suffering in prison was similar to what could be expected of hell was widespread in late antiquity" (*Prison, Punishment, and Penance*, 267).

14. Eusebius of Caesarea claims that during the Great Persecution Christians were dispatched to the mines at Phaeno (modern-day Khibet Faynan) in southwest Jordan as their punishment. Eusebius, *Hist. eccl.* 8.8, 10; *Mart. Pal.* 7.4; 8.1; Athanasius, *H. Ar.* 60.

frequently suffocated from noxious gases, were vulnerable to being crushed by piles of falling rocks, and were exposed to extreme heat and physical exhaustion.[15] These punishments played upon persistent ancient fears of sickness and disability that can be seen in the wide range of ancient thinkers (medical, philosophical, theological) who focused on how to attain and maintain the ideal body.

The ideal body in antiquity is also the masculine body. So hell's damned inhabit leaky, weak, disabled, and effeminate bodies. The overlap between disability and stigmatized femininity is not unique to antiquity, but has persisted to the present day. As pioneering Disability Studies scholar, Rosemarie Garland-Thomson argued in her work on 19th and 20th century "freak shows," "the non-normate status accorded disability feminizes all disabled figures," and again states, "Indeed the discursive equation of femaleness with disability is common, sometimes to denigrate women and sometimes to defend them."[16] Or as Jana Bennett has put it "the very fact of being a woman is a disability."[17] In short, the stigma associated with femininity is used to mark the disabled body as non-normative. In turn, association with disability impacts the cultural value of the female body. It is at this intersection between class, gender, disability, (and occasionally race), that the punishments of hell occur, leveraging intersecting forms of marginalization to depict the damned as the worst of the worst.

---

15. M. A. Perry, D. S. Coleman, D. L. Dettman, J. P. Grattan, and A. Halim al-Shiyab, "Condemned to Metallum? The Origin and Role of 4th–6th Century A.D. Phaeno Mining Camp Residents Using Multiple Chemical Techniques," *Journal of Archaeological Science* 38 (2011): 558–69. On Christian reflections on condemnation to the mines and the archeology of a North African prison, see M. D. C. Larsen, "Carceral Practices and Geographies in Roman North Africa: A Case Study," *SLA* 3, no. 4 (2019): 547–80; and M. Letteny and M. D. C. Larsen, "A Roman Prison at Lambaesis," *SLA* 5, no. 1 (2021): 65–102.

16. Rosemarie Garland-Thomson, *Extraordinary Bodies: Figuring Physical Disability in American Culture and Literature* (New York: Columbia University Press, 1997), 9, 19.

17. Jana Bennett, "Women, Disabled," in *Disability in the Christian Tradition: A Reader*, eds. Brian Brock and John Swinton (Grand Rapids, MI: Eerdmans, 2012), 427-41, at 427.

On earth the spectacle of these punishments generated fear that was thought to deter criminal behaviors and keep the enslaved and others of low-status in subjugation. In hell, these punishments were meant to scare everyone sinless. But in the process hell made disabled bodies emblematic of sin. In the *Apocalypse of Paul* blindness is a punishment for giving alms conspicuously, but not knowing God. This punishment makes concrete the links that ancient thinkers like Plato (*Timaeus* 45) made between vision, light, cognition, and the soul.[18] But the blind are not alone in the *Apocalypse of Paul*: they dwell alongside those with intestinal worms (a deadly and common illness), lacerated lips and tongues that impair speech, and amputated hands and feet. In early Christian hell the damned body is disabled and the disabled body is damned.

Dante uses different punishments, but he keeps alive the tradition of using elaborate descriptions of torture and impaired bodies to shame audiences into self-reflection. Bodies crying out in chronic pain, stung by hornets and wasps, eaten by worms, gasping for air or rolling around in smelly muck, like pigs (the punishment for gluttony) are on display as emblems of sin, all spectacles aimed at encouraging "self-control." In the eighth circle of hell Dante and Virgil see the "falsifiers," who are explicitly punished with disease, they "see the spirits lying heaped on one another in the dank bottom of that fetid valley. One lay gasping on another's shoulder, one on another's belly; and some were crawling on hands and knees among the broken boulders."[19] Here disease and disability are explicitly framed as punishments. Christian fantasies of torture like Dante's have kept alive for millennia the ancient Roman enslaver's ethics of social control and fixations on preserving a narrowly defined "ideal" body.

---

18. Lisa Trentin, "Exploring Visual Impairment in Ancient Rome," in *Disabilities in Roman Antiquity*, eds. Christian Laes, Chris Goodey, and M. Lynn Rose (Leiden, Netherlands: Brill, 2013), 89-114.

19. Dante *Inferno* Canto 29, translation by John Ciardi, *The Divine Comedy* (New York: New American Library, 2003).

Legacies of Oppression

We may want to congratulate ourselves on how far we have come from these scenes of fiery torture that reinforce ancient bodily norms and hold women disproportionately accountable for sexual encounters and family responsibilities. But a cursory glance at school dress codes reminds us that we are not so far removed from a world in which women's bodies are hypersexualized and policed. And U.S. maternity leave policies tell the story of a world in which women are expected to have children, and do the majority of the parenting, but receive very little support when they attempt to do so. The breast-feeding snakes are not as remote as we would like to imagine. It was in tours of hell that the bodies of women first become communal and public property. The legacy of these processes is still felt in modern society and decision making, but the gendered nature of hellish punishment continues to be overlooked in religious conversations about ethics.

As in Paul and Dante's hellscapes, the disabled body today is held up as a threat to the social ideals of self-control and health. In 2020 as the world grappled with the global pandemic the disabled body took center stage once again as the self-affirming image of the normative body. In the U.S., leaders who wanted to assure citizens of their safety used ableist language to do so, telling people that the virus would only be deadly for the elderly and those with pre-existing conditions. The not-so-subtle suggestion was there in plain sight: the deaths of persons with disabilities was preferable to economic collapse.[20]

After vaccines became available and many people gleefully declared the pandemic "over," the disability community has had new challenges to navigate, namely how to safely go to work, school, and the grocery store when only a portion of the population is vaccinated, many are not masked, and the vaccine is not effective

---

20. Doha Madani, " Dan Patrick on coronavirus: 'More important things than living'," *NBC News*, April 21, 2020, https://www.nbcnews.com/news/us-news/texas-lt-gov-dan-patrick-reopening-economy-more-important-things-n1188911

for the immunocompromised.[21] The global pandemic has at best placed increased socio-economic pressures on the disabled and at worst led to eugenicist cries for their death so that others can return to mask-less shopping with impunity.

For the so called able-bodied the pandemic has taken a different toll: persons with all manner of bodies find themselves to be vulnerable to something that they can't see, and public health measures heighten the collective awareness of bodily vulnerability—something that persons with disabilities have always known and defenders of the "normal body" work hard to ignore.[22] Disability studies scholars have argued that the disabled body makes the non-disabled uncomfortable because it reminds them of their own bodily vulnerability, that someday their body very likely will be disabled.[23] In the pandemic those who cling most tightly to the ideals of bodily invulnerability, resisting public health measures like masking, social distancing, and vaccination have proven again and again that this ableist myth is not only "toxic," it is deadly.[24]

Today few people are crafting Dante-esque hellscapes in which the disabled body symbolizes sin, but society has projected fears of the sick body onto disabled bodies and effectively placed the majority of the burden of the pandemic on those bodies. The disabled are forced to stay home, or left out of the public health conversation

21. Alice Wong (@SFdirewolf), Twitter, September 9, 2021, https://twitter.com/sfdirewolf/status/1435855758382432257

22. Julia Watts Belser, "Disability and the Politics of Vulnerability," *Berkley Forum,* April 15, 2020, https://berkleycenter.georgetown.edu/responses/disability-and-the-politics-of-vulnerability; Jana M. Bennet, "Disabilities in Hiding: How the Pandemic Might Shape Justice for All of Us," *Berkley Forum,* April 16, 2020, https://berkleycenter.georgetown.edu/responses/disabilities-in-hiding-how-the-pandemic-might-shape-justice-for-all-of-us.

23. Rosemarie Garland-Thomson has argued that "the disabled figure in cultural discourse assures the rest of the citizenry of who they are not while arousing their suspicions about who they could become" (*Extraordinary Bodies,* 41).

24. Rebecca Klar, "Va. bishop who defied social distancing recommendation dies of coronavirus complications," *The Hill,* April 14, 2020, https://thehill.com/homenews/state-watch/492653-virginia-bishop-who-was-defiant-of-coronavirus-dies-of-covid-19/; Hannah Frishberg, "Hillsong founder says vaccine is 'personal decision' after member dies of COVID," *New York Post,* July 26, 2021, https://nypost.com/2021/07/26/hillsong-founder-vaccines-are-personal-after-church-member-dies-of-covid/.

altogether.[25] In the exuberance to leave the pandemic behind we are creating a world in which "individual responsibility" allows us to gloss over our collective responsibilities to each other.

Time and again, our penchant for making hell has shown us that it favors the powerful, and carries both visible and hidden penalties for the marginalized. When we stop to consider how many of the earliest depictions of hell were focused on care for the marginalized other, hell's oppressive legacy is particularly stunning.[26] The "law of retaliation" that we find there seems in every way opposed to the ethic of non-retaliation of the Sermon on the Mount.[27] Christian hells centered Roman sexual ethics and tortures in ways that amplified the violence and hierarchical bodily standards of the ancient world. Contemporary society, like Dante, has not intervened in this violent legacy, but continues to imagine new spaces that penalize the marginalized body in a way that seems "fitting" according to the society that deemed it marginal. I have only offered a few examples here, but hopefully enough to show that we can be assured that human imaginations of justice are not God's justice. Imagining hell has imported the violence, patriarchy, ableism, and kyriarchy of the ancient world to the future for thousands of years. As we reflect on hell from many different angles in this volume, I suggest we take seriously the consequences of bringing these hells to earth.

---

25. Candida Moss, "I'm a Vaccinated Transplant Recipient. I Don't Have Antibodies. Now What?" *New York Times,* May 24, 2021, https://www.nytimes.com/2021/05/24/opinion/organ-transplant-covid-vaccine.html; Abdullah Shihipar (@AShihipar) "none of the mainstream pandemic plans/discourse really have an answer for what disabled and/or immunocompromised people should do until the pandemic ends. they are effectively erased from these plans," Twitter, September 9, 2021, https://twitter.com/AShihipar/status/1436175271460212737.

26. Matthew 25:31-46; Luke 16:19-31; Many of the punishments in the early Christian apocalypses are for those who did not follow the ethical rubric of the Sermon on the Mount: Apoc. Pet. 9; cf. Matt 5:3; Apoc. Pet. 9 and Apoc. Paul 44 cf. Matt 5:10-12; 6:24; Apoc. Pet. 12 and Apoc. Paul 40; cf. Matt 6:1-4; Apoc. Paul 31; cf. Matt 6:1-18; Apoc. Paul 39; cf. Matt 5:27-28.

27. Matthew 5:38-42.

CHAPTER 12

Into the Abyss: Mapping the Psychological Trauma of Hell Indoctrination

Mark G. Karris

Hell. It is just a four-letter word, and rather a small one compared to most words in the English dictionary. However, for many religious believers, and indeed some unbelievers, it is a word packed with explosive imagery and meaning.

Hell, and its associated eternal conscious torment (ECT), is viewed by many as a theological treasure that glorifies God. For them, given God's holiness and perfect justice, the concept of Hell makes perfect sense. One contemporary theologian puts it plainly, "to sin against an infinitely glorious being is an infinitely heinous offense that is worthy of an infinitely heinous punishment",[1] while another author and minister writes that "Hell is a terrifying place, but Hell glorifies God immensely because it makes so many of his qualities visible and knowable."[2] For these authors, Hell makes sense. God's holiness demands a verdict, and punishment must follow for those that sin. All that God creates and decrees is

---

1. Denny Burk, "Eternal Conscious Torment" in *Four Views on Hell: Second Edition,* ed. Preston M. Sprinkle (Grand Rapids, MI: Zondervan, 2016), 20.

2. Mark Ballenger, "How Does Hell Glorify God?," *Apply God's Word* (blog), December 27, 2016, https://applygodsword.com/how-does-hell-glorify-god/.

good and praiseworthy, and this necessarily includes Hell and the punishment of eternal conscious torment. Within this theological framework, trust in God's sovereignty and providence combined with the supposed designation of His followers as the "elect" mitigates against any feelings of anxiety or impending doom.

However, one's theological treasure is another's noxious trash. There are many who dissent from this interpretation of God and the afterlife, deeming it a horrific version of a wrathful punishing God. For these individuals, the idea of Hell likely generates terrifying images of an angry preacher, frothing at the mouth, loudly proclaiming a place created by God and filled with hideous and duplicitous demons, unceasing fire, unquenchable thirst, and never-ending torture.

Some with unveiled eyes move on quickly from what they consider to be a primitive view of God and religion. They tire of *fear and shame-based* religious propositions and decrees and the metaphysical niceties that fail to impact upon experiential realities. They abhor the Christian nationalism, misogynistic and patriarchal leadership, judgmental and venom-filled communities, and the vision of an ill-tempered and punitive God who is some sort of grotesque composite of Hitler, Stalin, and Mao Zedong. They walk away and move forward, letting the past be the past and feeling more alive than ever!

Others who walk away from this toxic religious matrix can find themselves stuck. There is a sense that, although their core self has escaped the religious trauma they experienced, the inability to move forward remains. It's like a frustrating sludge holds them back, keeping them from living the life of freedom they desire. While they no longer must deny, suppress, or repress their doubts and troublesome questions regarding toxic beliefs, they continue to feel emotionally shaken, unable to experience themselves as an integrated, whole self. They have been traumatized by toxic religion.

There are numerous potentially traumatizing aspects of religion, but this chapter focuses specifically on the psychological terrain and trauma associated with the religious doctrine of Hell and eternal conscious torment. Although Hell-related trauma can have myriad effects, due to the need for brevity, the chapter will pay special attention to the harmful outcomes of debilitating anxiety, toxic shame, and negative self-criticism. Most importantly, I will incorporate the experiences of those who have suffered from the theology of original sinful hell-bound people, as their voices are perhaps the clearest expression of this trauma and deserve to be heard.

What is Trauma?

The word "trauma" derives from the Greek word for *wound* or *injury*, and "psyche" is the Latin word for *soul.* We can combine these words to get the clinical term "psychological trauma" and the poetic phrase "soul wound."[3] Events likely to create soul wounds include abuse of various kinds: war, mass shootings, domestic violence, and natural disasters. Soul wounds often involve actual or feared death, or serious emotional or physical injury.

Who among us has not experienced trauma? We live in a culture of trauma within a traumatized world. Trauma and vicarious trauma—being negatively affected by witnessing others' trauma— is part of the air we breathe. Each of us carries soul wounds that deeply affect our minds, bodies, and nervous systems. The magnitude of people's soul wounds varies, of course, as do the origins of them. A soul wound may result from a single event, while "complex trauma" goes beyond one-time incidents and involves more pervasive exposure to traumatic experiences.

Traumatic events can have devastating consequences for our physiology, spirituality, and relationality. Importantly, there are individual differences in the perception and experience of trauma. The same event can be perceived as traumatic by one person but not another. Each individual's reaction to potentially traumatic

---

3. See Russ Harris, *Trauma-Focused Act: A Practitioner's Guide to Working with Mind, Body, and Emotion Using Acceptance and Commitment Therapy* (Oakland, CA: New Harbinger Publications, 2022), 2.

events is determined by a plethora of complex interrelated factors including their upbringing, genetics, temperament, coping strategies, support network, home environment, and current life stressors.

When we do not have enough internal or external resources to adequately cope with traumatic events, then the psychological and physiological responses to trauma can continue and develop into post-traumatic stress disorder (PTSD). Complex PTSD (C-PTSD), which is what I would categorize for most religious trauma, has three overarching categories of symptoms that include (1) re-experiencing if the traumatic event through intrusive memories, nightmares, or flashbacks; (2) avoidance of experiences related to the trauma; and (3) pervasive feelings of hypervigilance and a nervous system that perceives that peril is right around the corner.

Religious Trauma

Dr. Marlene Winell is a well-known pioneer in the field of religious trauma and the author of *Leaving the Fold: A Guide to Former Fundamentalists and Others Leaving Their Religion*. Winell uses the term "Religious Trauma Syndrome" to describe the aftereffects of toxic religious experience. She writes: "Leaving a religion after total immersion can cause a complete upheaval of a person's construction of reality, including the self, other people, life, and the future. People unfamiliar with this situation, including therapists, have trouble appreciating the sheer terror it can create."[4]

Reba Riley, who has written about her faith deconstruction journey, calls the experience "Post-Traumatic Church Syndrome".[5] Riley writes emphatically about the destructive side effects of

---

4. Valerie Tarico, "Religious Trauma Syndrome: Psychologist reveals how organized religion can lead to mental health problems," *Raw Story,* September 5, 2019, https://www.rawstory.com/2019/09/religious-trauma-syndrome-psychologist-reveals-how-organized-religion-can-lead-to-mental-health-problems/.

5. See Reba Riley, *Post-Traumatic Church Syndrome: One Woman's Desperate, Funny, and Healing Journey to Explore 30 Religions by Her 30th Birthday* (New York: Howard Books, 2016).

religious trauma, which include: "…anger, grief, despair, depression, failure to believe in anything, moral confusion, loss of gravity, and emptiness."[6] A more academic definition of religious trauma is given by the North American Committee on Religious Trauma Research (NACRTR), who characterize it as follows:

> "Religious trauma results from an event, series of events, relationships, or circumstances within or connected to religious beliefs, practices, or structures that is experienced by an individual as overwhelming or disruptive and has lasting adverse effects on a person's physical, mental, social, emotional, or spiritual well-being."[7]

The Traumatic Effects of Hell Indoctrination

There are diverse perspectives on the subject of Hell. Some Christians, for example, have been taught about Hell but have always thought it a strange idea and chosen not to accept it. They have perhaps not thought about the concept too deeply and hold no particularly strong feelings about it. Then there are people who believe in Hell and are sad that it exists, yet feel no anxiety as they believe they are *the elect*, and therefore in no danger of hellfire.

For others, belief in Hell comes with a drop of narcissistic pride. They are glad that it exists, and feel no anxiety because they believe they are *the righteous,* thus will be saved from Hell. There are also those who believe in a Hell that does not involve eternal conscious torment. This group might meditate on the nature of Hell as a place of purification, or as a space where one comes away with not, "a servile fear of a cruel and merciless god, but with a new image of God, a God of infinite patience, humility, and love".[8]

---

6. Ibid., 10

7. "Religious Trauma Research." Global Center for Religious Research. Accessed September 10, 2022. https://www.gcrr.org/religioustrauma.

8. Eric Jensen, "Hell and the Image of God in the Spiritual Exercises," *The Way* 57, no. 4 (2018): 91–102. https://search.ebscohost.com/login.aspx?direct=true&db=aph&AN =130667933&site=ehost-live&scope=site.

This is just a small sample of the range of experiences people have when they think of Hell. There are, of course, many more. For the moment, let us focus on how Hell affects those who experience it as traumatic. I especially want to present to the reader some voices on the margins of this painful reality.

The Trauma of Original Sinful Hell-Bound People (OSHBP)

The doctrine of Hell is deeply connected to the doctrine of Original Sin and a view that human beings are unclean and repulsive to a holy and perfect God. Under a premise I refer to as *Original Sinful Hell-Bound People* (OSHBP), humans have zero worth in and of ourselves. We are objects deserving of wrath, and there is nothing good within us or about us. Taking this theology to its logical conclusion, even the believers in ECT who wax poetic on God loving us must accept that it cannot be *us* who God loves. According to OSHBP, God cannot even look at us without wanting to send us into the pit of hell, because we are evil (a common belief that even Jesus alluded to in Luke 11:13). This narrative proposes that because we are so repugnant before God, He can only see us through the prism of Jesus. God's disgust and wrath toward us is absorbed in Christ. So, humans are nothing, and Christ is everything.

The pathological ramifications of indoctrinating followers (and children who can't even consent to following a religious path) with the message of OSHBP, and its related idea of eternal torture, are grievous. Such toxic theologies have the potential to create monumental soul wounds, with reverberations so insidious and destructive that their effects may take many years from which to recover.

Let us now explore the negative consequences of the C-PTSD following the religious trauma of Hell indoctrination.

Hell Anxiety

To date there has been sparse scientific research into Hell-related trauma. Researchers have, however, coined the term *Hell anxiety*, to encapsulate the experience of apprehension many have in relation to Hell. They have also created a questionnaire, named the "Hell Anxiety Scale," to measure it.[9] The scale is comprised of nine statements, with respondents asked to indicate how much each statement applies to them. For example, one statement is, 1.) "Sometimes it's difficult to control my worry about Hell." Another is, 2.) "I feel an intense fear of Hell when I do something I'm not supposed to do." Lastly, 3.) "I am fearful when ministers and other religious authorities talk about Hell."

One study, conducted at Baylor University, concluded that "People who fear Hell are some of the most anxious Americans."[10] Another showed that priming, or having participants think about Hell by attending to relevant prompts, "leads to lower levels of positive emotion and higher levels of negative emotion, compared to controls."[11] These conclusions are straightforward enough: thinking about a God who can cause extreme torment in one's afterlife for not living up to His perceived standards in this life can cause profound psychological responses, including negative feelings and overwhelming anxiety.

To supplement this information from the ivory tower, it is crucial to hear people's lived experiences with religious trauma and the effects of Hell anxiety. Charlotte, a woman discussed in Marlene

9. Stephen Cranney, Joseph Leman, Thomas A. Fergus, and Wade C. Rowatt, "Hell Anxiety Scale," *APA PsycTests*, (January 2018) doi:10.1037/t72689-000.

10. "American Values, Mental Health, and Using Technology in the Age of Trump" Baylor Religion Survey Wave 5, September 2017, https://www.baylor.edu/BaylorReligionSurvey/index.php?id=942305.

11. Azim F. Shariff and Lara B. Aknin, "The Emotional Toll of Hell: Cross-National and Experimental Evidence for the Negative Well-Being Effects of Hell Beliefs," *PLoS ONE* 9, no. 1 (2014) doi:10.1371/journal.pone.0085251.

Winell's book *Leaving the Fold,* described her intense Hell anxiety and stated:

> "They quoted the scripture about the camel that can't get through the eye of a needle, so even one little sin can't get into heaven. So even though I was a real good kid, every time that I thought anything bad or felt anything that I thought was bad or did anything that somebody else thought was bad, I automatically thought that if I died at that moment, I'd go to Hell. Even though I had already accepted Jesus and went to church and did everything I was supposed to do, I had nightmares and was always anxious. I went up to the altar all the time to ask forgiveness."[12]

This overwhelming sense of Hell Anxiety has been elucidated by Dennis Gunnarson, author of *Fostering a Healthy Soul: Escaping Spiritual Disillusionment.* He writes, "Growing up in the church, the message of eternal punishment was vividly presented. I responded to the altar call for salvation almost every week. I was afraid I would go to Hell if I didn't."[13] One young woman from the *Bielefeld-Based Cross-Cultural Study,* in which people who had de-converted from Christianity were examined, shared her anxiety about whether to date a non-Christian. She recalls thinking to herself, *"You're not gonna be happy; you're gonna live a life of evil; Satan will have a hold of you; and you'll basically burn in Hell in the afterlife."*[14] The same theme is expressed by Krispin Mayfield, author of *Attached to God,* who wrote:

---

12. Quoted in Marlene Winell, *Leaving the Fold* (Berkeley, CA: Apocryphile, 2007), 63.

13. Dennis Gunnarson, "Fostering a Healthy Soul: Escaping Spiritual Disillusionment" (Independently Published, 2022), 95.

14. Heinz Streib, Ralph W. Hood, Barbara Keller, Rosina-Martha Csoff, and Christopher F. Silver, *Deconversion: Qualitative and Quantitative Results from Cross Cultural Research in Germany and the United States of America* (Germany: Vandenhoeck & Ruprecht, 2009), 101.

I've always been terrified of Hell. I could never quite relax with God because I always worried…that in the end it'd turn out I was a goat, not a sheep. This fear has always hung over my head, causing me to white-knuckle my spiritual life. What if I didn't have true faith? What if, between now and my death, I made some terrible decisions or ended up renouncing my faith? As much as I wanted to feel safe in the everlasting arms, I knew that I wasn't. If anyone could go to Hell, then I could go to Hell, which meant I could never relax.[15]

Thus far, research into Hell Anxiety has tended to focus on the individual's anxious feelings about their own future state. However, there is also evidence of intense worry being expressed about *others* experiencing eternal conscious torment. As one participant in a study detailed in the research paper, *The Resurrection of Self*, put it:

You wake up in the night screaming because you're afraid your mama's going to Hell. Or I'm going to Hell, or even though I was baptized, what if I don't really believe, or I've committed this sin, does that mean I'm not really a Christian and I've gotta go find uncle so and so who doesn't go to church because he might die and he will go to Hell.[16]

Trauma's Imprint on the Body

Those who have never experienced religious trauma may find it hard to understand the ripple effects that such trauma can have on the bodies and nervous systems of those who have soul wounds due to their belief in Hell. This is not just a matter of struggling

---

15. Krispin Mayfield, *Attached to God: A Practical Guide to Deeper Spiritual Experience* (Grand Rapids, MI: Zondervan, 2022), 198.

16. Amy Phillips, "The Resurrection of Self: How Deconversion from Religious Belief to Atheism Healed a History of Rejection, Trauma, and Shame," *Dissertation Abstracts International Section A: Humanities and Social Sciences* 77, no. 3 (2016): 160.

with beliefs, or a dilemma of the mind. Rather, such trauma can set in motion a cascade of negative effects throughout the body, and become a profoundly physiological and emotional dilemma, not merely a cognitive one. Bessel van der Kolk, an expert on trauma, writes:

> Traumatized people chronically feel unsafe inside their bodies. The past is alive in the form of gnawing interior discomfort. Their bodies are constantly bombarded by visceral warning signs, and, in an attempt to control these processes, they often become expert at ignoring their gut feelings and in numbing awareness of what is played out inside. They learn to hide from their selves.[17]

A deep dive into the neurobiology of the trauma of Hell is not necessary here. The sufferer's experience can be described in simple terms. Whether the trauma occurred during the first encounter with the doctrine of Hell or at some later point, it produced an absolute shock of fear that sent stress hormones surging through the victim's body and nervous system. The encounter with the idea of a powerful God who believes that the individual is a depraved sinner deserving of being tortured in Hell for eternity no doubt left a traumatic imprint on their brains and bodies.

Why? Because the brain's main purpose is to keep us alive and free from pain. This imprint can be seen as similar to the one left when touching a hot stove when young. The shock leaves behind a constant reminder: "Fear the stove! DO NOT TOUCH!" Regarding Hell, it would say: "Fear God! DO NOT SIN!"

One of the consequences of religious C-PTSD is that, after experiencing it, we never truly feel at home in our bodies again. Due to evolutionary processes, our brains are already geared towards self-protection. Add to this a need to constantly be on alert

---

17. Bessel van der Kolk, *The Body Keeps the Score: Brain, Mind, and Body in the Healing of Trauma* (New York: Penguin, 2015), 96.

about our and others' eternal fate, and the result is a diminished capacity to experience the comfort that comes with activation of our brain's *"tend and befriend"* or *care-circuit,* the part of our nervous system that gives us warm and positive feelings. Instead, the *fight-or-flight* system is constantly activated, putting us into a state of hyperarousal with associated physical reactions, such as muscle tension, upset stomach, fatigue, dizziness, rapid heart rate, teeth grinding, and chronic pain.

Shame and Self-Criticism

Two of the most negative and harmful aspects of C-PTSD following the religious trauma of Hell indoctrination are shame and its common bedfellow, self-criticism. Although most researchers differentiate between guilt and shame, there is surprisingly no consensus concerning their exact definitions.

Guilt is commonly understood as a cognitive and emotional experience that individuals feel after they perceive they have done something wrong. It is focused on behavior and the negative implications of that behavior. Those who feel guilty typically experience remorse. If the guilt is due to one's actions towards others, the guilty party is often motivated to repair the harmed relationship. *Shame,* on the other hand, is focused almost exclusively on the self. Moreover, toxic shame causes individuals to believe that they *are* something wrong or that they are flawed, inferior, or tainted in some way.

Lewis Smedes explains that shame is, "a vague, undefined heaviness that presses on our spirit, dampens our gratitude for the goodness of life, and slackens the free flow of joy. Shame...seeps into and discolors all our other feelings, primarily about ourselves, but about almost everyone and everything else in our life as well."[18]

---

18. Lewis B. Smedes, *Shame and Grace: Healing the Shame We Don't Deserve* (San Francisco: Harper San Francisco, 1993), 1.

Unhealed shame is one of the most harmful emotions humans can experience, especially if it is left to fester and darken one's own self-view, as well as their views on God and other people. Hell trauma and the consequence of shame is a contributing factor that contributes to intense emotional suffering and may catapult individuals into addiction, self-harm, or be a factor in harming others. I define religious shame as: "An intense and lasting neurobiological imprint that was formed in a religious context that perpetually affects a person's core identity (e.g., worthlessness, unlovability, etc.) and decreases their overall quality of life".

Shame arising from Hell trauma can be a potent contributor to intense emotional suffering, and may catapult individuals into addiction, self-harm, or harming others. When a pastor warns that a powerful God will throw you into the pit of Hell because of your sin, he is heaping feelings of religious shame upon you. When parents tell their children, "Don't do that; God is watching, and, God doesn't like disobedience," they are burdening their child with religious shame. When a youth pastor uses the Bible to condemn and harshly judge those who are working through and integrating their sexuality, they are injecting them with poisonous religious shame.

Shame often leads to paralyzing self-criticism. While a degree of self-criticism can be useful and even beneficial, too much can quickly become harmful. Self-criticism is strongly related to a host of psychopathologies, such as anxiety, anger and aggression, depression, perfectionism, and self-harm. One popular view of self-criticism has been detailed by Gilbert, who describes it as the tendency to engage in self-judgment, directed toward different aspects of the self, including behaviors, emotions, thoughts, and performance.[19] Gilbert notes that there are different forms of self-criticism. For some, it involves feeling small, incapable, and inferior, while for others it may be connected to self-hatred due to past trauma.

---

19. Paul Gilbert, *Compassion Focused Therapy: Distinctive Features.* (London, UK: Routledge, 2010).

I define religious self-criticism as the "negative evaluation of the self, based on repeated contact with past religious propositions, practices, policies, and persons." Here are some shame-based self-critical statements from people I have worked with due to their OSHBP-related trauma:

- "I feel tainted. I deserve to be alone."

- "I feel horrible about myself. People don't want me. God doesn't even want me."

- "I feel like I did something wrong for this to happen. Truth is, there were a lot of sinful things I did in my life. God is probably right to punish me."

- "I deserve to go to Hell."

- "God hates me for being gay. I don't want to burn in Hell."

- "God loves everyone else but me."

- "I am sinful and no good. Any good that I have is like a filthy rag."

- "I am unloved. What is the point of living?"

- "I am terrible for deconstructing my faith. I am nervous that I will bring my family along with me."

An account of how the trauma of Hell and its related doctrines leads to shame, self-criticism, and other negative effects can be made clearer using personal testimony. One participant in a qualitative research study on religious trauma in sexual minority clients shared this about his anxiety about himself and God:

I learned that He couldn't be around me because I was permanently unholy. I learned that anyone who wasn't straight was an abomination destined for hell, and that even if I was saved and would go to heaven, I would still be separated from God because I was unholy. God couldn't have me near Him even in heaven.[20]

David, a friend of mine, shared with me his own experiences of Hell trauma, relaying to me, "Mark, I was raised as a Pentecostal Christian. I constantly heard how my righteousness was as filthy rags. I was constantly made to feel that with each lustful look, every thought about myself in a positive way, and each prideful glance God can send me to hell in an instant."

A study exploring the mechanisms of religious trauma among young LGBTQIA+ people detailed their accounts of feeling intense shame and constant dread about the fires of Hell. The researchers wrote, "The intensity of rhetoric directed against them imbues a deep fear of the sexual dimensions of their identity, perpetuating cycles of shame and self-loathing that frame their whole sense of self."[21] Matthew Distefano, in his book *Learning to Float*, writes:

And then there were the questions about God's nature. Why was his solution to my sin so archaic? Hell? Really? Eternal torment? Violence to the nth degree? Abandonment times a trillion? I had a dad who left me when I was at my most vulnerable so why did I need a heavenly father who was the exact same? He is the one who made me, right? Then why was he going to hold my ineptitude against me for all eternity?[22]

Unhealed shame can be one of the most harmful emotions a human can experience, especially if it is left to fester and darken

---

20. Seth C. Crocker, "Persevering Faith: A Qualitative Exploration of Religious Trauma and Spiritual Resilience in Sexual Minority Christians," *Dissertation Abstracts International: Section B: The Sciences and Engineering* (2022).

21. Joel Hollier, Shane Clifton, and Jennifer Smith-Merry, "Mechanisms of Religious Trauma amongst Queer People in Australia's Evangelical Churches," *Clinical Social Work Journal* 50, no. 3 (2022): 275–85. doi:10.1007/s10615-022-00839-x.

22. Matthew Distefano and Michelle Collins, preface to *Learning to Float* (Quoir, 2022).

one's self-view, as well as one's views of God and others. It is unthinkable, yet sadly frequently observable, that the debilitating feeling that one is unlovable, tainted, dirty, and no good, and the toxic fuel this provides to the inner critic, originates from a religion promoting freedom and abundance.

The Lasting Effects of The Trauma of Hell

As many people can attest, tenacious views about original sin and Hell can linger even after deconverting and changing one's beliefs. Philips writes about this phenomenon based on the experiences of his participants, "The fear of hell was a concern that was so hard to overcome, that respondents experienced it throughout their deconversion and even after loss of belief had occurred."[23] Such occurrences raise the question as to why these dastardly doctrines are so stubborn and difficult to discard?

Beliefs linked to the trauma of Hell persist not so much because they are true, but because they are so vile and horrific that our nervous system encodes them as perpetual possible threats. The brain, and in particular the amygdala, carries the anxiety-producing message, "Even though I don't believe it now, I don't want to forget it, just in case it is true." This primitive part of our brain is not necessarily concerned with what is objectively accurate, as it functions only to keep us alive and protect us from pain.

Choosing to no longer believe in original sin and Hell is like telling the brain after a lion attack that happened years ago, "You remember that ferocious lion, well that really wasn't a lion (even though you have scars to suggest otherwise)." Sufferers of Hell trauma were told by those in authority, God's mouthpieces, that God thinks we are depraved sinners deserving of being tortured for eternity. It is hard to just forget those instances and the absolute traumatic shock of fear that initially rushed through our nervous system.

---

23. Amy Phillips, "The Resurrection of Self", 49.

Continually being reminded of these doctrines by Christians carrying hate- and hell-filled picket signs, or by angry preachers threatening fire and brimstone on television, hardly helps. These can all act as cues, or triggers, setting off an immediate emotional reaction. While the neocortex, the brain's evolutionarily newer region typically associated with rational thought, might assure us that the doctrine of Original Sinful Hell-Bound People is illogical nonsense, the more primitive part of the brain where fearful memories are stored (the amygdala and dorsal hippocampus) can be easily triggered to remind us that God-created nightmares are probably true. Since the amygdala doesn't have a sense of time, each memory can feel like the first time you experienced the terrifying shock of the original fear-based teaching.

Conclusion

My hope is that readers can take away from this chapter the absolute seriousness of religious soul wounds and the potentially scarring effects of the doctrines of Hell and the interrelated doctrine of original sinful human beings. Even those with expertise in this area would have to admit that we have only just scratched the surface when it comes to understanding the profound consequences of such indoctrination.

Anxiety, shame, and self-criticism are just some of the potentially devastating effects of poisonous theological ideas and religious trauma. To think that Jesus came to preach good news to the poor, proclaim freedom for prisoners, open the eyes of the blind, release the oppressed, and proclaim the year of God's favor for all (Luke 4:18-19), yet that many people's encounters with Christianity have left them with bad news, bondage, blindness to their own beauty, and a belief in a punitive God who, at some level, abhors all humans, is truly tragic.[24]

---

24. As a therapist, I do believe in hope and healing for religious trauma. This chapter is taken from my forthcoming book, tentatively titled *Out of the Fiery Abyss: Healing from the Trauma of Hell Indoctrination*. It will be released in 2023.

CHAPTER 13

A Young Pastor's Journey in Deconstruction

Josh Patterson

Why I Value (But Also Dislike) Deconstruction

It is no secret that deconstruction has become a popular topic amongst the various Christian communities today. Unfortunately, deconstruction has become just one more thing that is dividing the Body of Christ and polarizing our churches, its scholars and its congregants. It seems to me that one falls either as a conservative looking down their nose at all of those "progressive" and "woke" individuals who find themselves participating in the "slippery slope" that is deconstruction, or one falls as a progressive who is clearly above and smarter than all of those power-hungry and oppressive conservatives.

Now here's the thing…there are deep truths embedded in both of these perspectives and viewpoints. There are deep patriarchal, racist and oppressive ideas baked into a lot of the theological doctrines and traditions that so many of us have grown up with. There is no doubt that theology has been used to oppress entire people groups, justify slavery, support colonization, dehumanize those who look different than us, oppress women, justify violence and support Christian nationalism. None of these things are okay. In fact, I would argue that all the above-mentioned ways that theology has been used are inherently anti-Christ; that is, they are the antithesis of the message of Jesus. They oppose the very thing Jesus came to do.

However, it is also true that there is a lot of hubris and arrogance to be found within the more progressive Christian circles. As somebody who tends to find themselves firmly within a more progressive camp, I find it only fair to critique our shortcomings as well... and trust me, there are many. The more progressive crowd does tend to ignore individuals and focus solely on larger systems. Progressives also run the risk of becoming so tolerant, they become intolerant. Much of this has to do with the fact that many progressives are still fundamentalists, they just fall on the other side of the fence now, so to speak. Their failure to learn HOW to think instead of just WHAT to think all the time leads to countless pointless arguments and a deep display of arrogance and condescending behaviors.

Within my experience, conservatives tend link everything to individuals and their sins whereas progressives link everything to the larger systems at play in the world. I tend to find it rather axiomatic that humans have the acute ability to really screw things up, so perhaps the conservatives are actually right. However, I also find it rather obvious that systems exist that favor and privilege one people group (namely educated, white, cisgender males) over everybody else... so perhaps the progressives are right.

Both the individual and the systemic present great problems that need to be addressed. When we simply challenge the individual, we are missing out on the larger entities (read principalities and powers) at play in the world, and therefore only address one half of the issue. At the same time, when we only focus on the oppressive and abusive systems of the world, we tend to forget about the individuals who are involved and again fail to address the whole issue. When we only focus on changing systems and not transforming the people who make up those systems, we will only continue to perpetuate harmful systems. As mature adults we need to learn how to bring together paradoxes and hold these two seemingly contradictory ideas together in tension. It is only then that we can genuinely move forward in a way that is true, helpful and deeply holistic.

All that to say, I am not a fan of the term deconstruction, although I get it. I used the term for a long time and most people would probably place my podcast in the category of "deconstruction podcasts"... I mean I was asked to write a chapter on deconstruction for crying out loud! I don't want to write off the word completely, I simply want to point out that it is helpful until it's not.

The idea of deconstructing can be insanely helpful and, dare I say, necessary. After all, a static faith is a dead faith and an unquestioned faith quickly falls into idolatry. Every issue I listed above should be more than enough evidence for us to agree that there are ideas, doctrines and theologies that NEED to be deconstructed. As Christians we have been told that people will know us by our love and that everything should be tested by its fruits.[1] The fruits of the spirit are love, joy, peace, patience, kindness, goodness, faithfulness, gentleness and self-control.[2] Any teaching or doctrine that does not produce this kind of fruit should be questioned and deconstructed.

Many things in scripture are not clear, but Jesus did seem to be pretty clear when he was asked which of the commandments is the greatest.

"Jesus replied: "'Love the Lord your God with all your heart and with all your soul and with all your mind.' This is the first and greatest commandment. And the second is like it: 'Love your neighbor as yourself.' All the Law and the Prophets hang on these two commandments."
—Matthew 22: 37-40

---

1. John 13:35, Matthew 7:16
2. Gal. 5:22-23

Here we see Jesus tying the idea of loving God and loving neighbor together... If we love God, we will also love our neighbor. Failing to love our neighbor is a failure to love God. Any doctrine or ideology that does not result in love of neighbor and love of God NEEDS to be deconstructed.

So what then is my issue with deconstruction? Ultimately, I have a few issues with the way deconstruction is approached and talked about. For starters, it seems to be an inherently negative word. It seems to imply that the process we call "deconstruction" is a negative process. I would much rather just call this process spiritual growth. If you are asking questions and seeking answers to the biggest questions of faith and what it means to be human, you are growing not backsliding. The movement is positive and forward, not negative and backward.

Richard Rohr describes this movement as "the wisdom pattern."[3] This pattern can be found throughout various faith traditions and philosophies, even though they may use different language to describe it. In Christianity, we talk about the pattern this way: life, death, resurrection. Walter Brueggemann teaches this through the Psalms with Psalms of Orientation, Psalms of Disorientation, Psalms of New Orientation.[4] Rohr calls it Order, Disorder, Reorder.[5]

Regardless of what language you prefer, my point is simply this—asking questions, changing your mind and growing in wisdom are all parts of a healthy spirituality and faith. We don't have to frame our growth in negative ways if we don't want to. If the word deconstruction works for you, great, I don't want to take that from you. However, I personally like to talk about spiritual growth and maturity.

---

3. Richard Rohr, *The Wisdom Pattern: Order—Disorder—Reorder* (London: SPCK, 2022).

4. Walter Brueggemann, *Spirituality of the Psalms* (Minneapolis: Augsburg, 2001).

5. Rohr, *Wisdom Pattern*.

My Deconstruction Journey

When it comes to deconstruction, there have been many theories put out there as to why people deconstruct their beliefs. Most often these theories are being propagated by "authority figures" within the Christian tradition who have not actually experienced deconstruction for themselves. It has been said by such people that deconstruction is simply a "sexy fad" and that people are deconstructing simply because they want to sin.

In my experience, and in the experience of others who actually have experienced deconstruction, I do not believe this to be the case. People don't choose to deconstruct their belief system, it's more so something that just happens. It is also a deeply painful and scary experience to go through. To call into question one's worldview and entire system of belief is a frightening experience that turns one's entire world upside down.

As I look back over my own journey of faith, it occurs to me that the cracks in my faith that ultimately lead to my deconstruction experience began much earlier and in a much less anticipated way than I had originally thought. The cracks in my faith started after reading "Surprised by Hope: Rethinking Heaven, the Resurrection, and the Mission of the Church" by N.T. Wright[6] during my Senior year of college. It was the reading of this book that broke the Heaven/Hell framework I had been given growing up and that led to my deep love of theology.

After graduating college, I had a short stint working for an Evangelical parachurch organization that worked with youth. During my first week on the job, tragedy struck and three students from my assigned High School were killed in a car crash. Coming face-to-face with death and tragedy and engaging with students who were not necessarily Christian began to deepen the cracks within my theological framework. Was I really supposed to tell these mourning teenagers that everything happens for a reason?

---

6. N.T. Wright, *Surprised by Hope* (London: SPCK, 2011).

Was I really supposed to tell them that this was all a part of God's plan? Was I really supposed to tell them that their deceased friends were now suffering in Hell because they didn't check the "right" theological boxes during their short time on this earth? It was this moment in time that led me to discover "The Uncontrolling Love of God: An Open And Relational Account Of Providence" by Thomas Jay Oord.[7]

It was also during my time with this organization that I began to have questions about the Bible. I had grown up being taught inerrancy and was also being mentored at that time by a PCA pastor who was teaching me the same thing. I had questions about the Bible that my pastor friend could not answer, in fact he didn't want to answer them and so he introduced me to somebody who is now both a close friend and mentor, Jace. Although Jace is much more conservative than I am, Jace opened the doors of Biblical Scholarship to me. He allowed me to ask the difficult questions and even pointed me in the direction of some deeply helpful books including the work of Pete Enns.[8] Here too another crack in my evangelical system of belief began to develop.

After being at the parachurch organization for one short school year, my wife and I moved to South Florida where I took a job as a Teaching Pastor at a church in Boca Raton. Working in this church was really where my deconstruction journey took on new heights and depths. I continued to study theology, reading books in my free time and listening to nerdy podcasts during my commute. I could write an entire memoir about my experience at this church, but for the sake of time simply know the following—during my time at this church I experienced verbal, emotional, spiritual and border-line physical abuse at the hands of the lead pastor. I only spent a total of 8 months at this church, but it seemed to me like a

---

7. Thomas Jay Oord, *The Uncontrolling Love of God: An Open and Relational Account of Providence* (Downers Grove, IL: InterVarsity, 2015).

8. Peter Enns, *The Bible Tells Me So: Why Defending Scripture Has Made Us Unable to Read It* (San Francisco, CA: HarperOne, 2015).

lifetime. It was there in Boca Raton that I developed a deep depression and dealt with extreme anxiety daily.

Oddly enough, this situation did not cause me to want to walk away from Christianity but actually pushed me to study more and grow deeper in my theological knowledge so that I could prove the people at this church wrong. After leaving the church in Boca, I took a job at a Methodist church in West Palm Beach. This church was a much better experience for sure, however, it still had some pretty big issues. Although this church served the community well and had an overall good orthopraxy, the staff culture was a mess! Suffice it to say that the toxic and damaging staff culture only furthered my depression and also was the straw that broke the camel's back, pushing me over the line and leading me to question the Church as an institution and eroding my trust in pastors and other 'spiritual authorities'.

It was during my time at the Methodist church that I decided to launch my podcast which at the time was called "Theology Doesn't Suck!". I set out to have deep conversations with my friend Andy who held vastly different theological perspectives than I did. Starting this podcast led me to continue my study of theology and church history. I began interacting with some of my favorite theologians and biblical scholars seeking out answers to all of my questions. The work I have done with this podcast over the past 3 or so years has been a public display of my own theological journey.

An interesting development in my faith happened at this Methodist church that I am deeply grateful for. It was there that I was given permission to be fully open and affirming to the LGBTQ+ community. This was a very live question for me on a deeply personal level. My family was kicked out of our Southern Baptist church when my brother Jordan came out to our family. Jordan was in seventh grade at the time and I was in my freshman year of high school. When things first happened, I embraced a celibacy position in regard to the LGBTQ+ community and my brother.

Fast forward back to the Methodist church where I met one of my best friends Chad, the Director of Modern Worship, who also just happened to be an openly gay man. My friendship with Chad and my experience of Chad within a vocational ministry context gave me what I needed to become fully accepting and affirming. I learned from this experience that theology is not just abstract concepts and ideas, but rather theology has deep impacts on the life of those around you. Seeing Chad in a loving and committed relationship with another man AND leading deeply spirit-filled worship on Sundays broke open and destroyed what I had been taught about those within the LGBTQ+ community. Relationships matter. Theology is also always biography.

After about 1.5 years working at the Methodist Church, I was pretty fed up with the antics and toxic culture. Noelle and I decided to move back home to Maryland where I would give working in a church one last chance. Luckily for me, the church I was hired at was amazing and easily the best church context I had ever worked in. It was here that my theological questioning was celebrated and allowed. It was also here that I discovered what a healthy church culture could look like. Unfortunately for me, the damage was already done. My mistrust of the church and of spiritual leaders caused issues for me internally. Even though I was allowed to ask questions, I never felt that I was able to say what I really thought or believed.

I felt like an outcast. At one point I was involved with a group of youth pastors that would get together from our area. During one of the meetings, I was asked about my opinion on hell. Instead of giving a straight answer, I decided instead to simply present the three live options that have been given within Christian history. After doing so these youth pastors decided to go behind my back. They emailed and texted parents at my church telling them that I was unsafe and that they should not allow their kids to attend youth group with me. I had students being texted by other students telling them that I was a heretic and my teachings were dangerous.

My internal world and my external world were at odds. My continued study of theology was taking me into places that were not allowed and celebrated within my context. I started to feel like a fake and a liar. I could not really get up and share where I was and what I was going through because it would not be fair to my students or the other pastors on staff. I entered into what was my first real "dark night of the soul." Luckily, I was connected with a spiritual director at the time who helped me immensely.

Part of my issue was that I had conflated my identity with my vocation. I also had conflated my beliefs with my identity. My spiritual director helped walk me through this difficult period in my life when I started to consider leaving vocational ministry. It was also during this time that I began to engage in spiritual practices such as centering prayer. I began to find a home amongst the mystics and eventually found the courage to walk away from vocational ministry.

It's a long story, but I ended up where I am now, working as a brewer for a local craft brewery here in Baltimore. Much has happened in my spiritual walk since leaving the church including a period of time where I stopped podcasting and entered into another deep and scary "dark night of the soul." For the sake of time, allow me to share with you the introduction to my podcast to give you an idea of where I find myself today:

> *"All of us are on a journey of becoming… a never-ending journey in pursuit of truth and deeper union with the Divine. Many of you know that faith is a complicated thing and that our journey of becoming can be both difficult and painful. Far too often we have not been given a space where we can safely address the complications and issues that arise naturally.*
>
> *My name is Joshua Patterson. My good friend Greg Farrand and I are also on this journey of becoming. We are both dedicated to inviting you into our journeys and creating a space where questions and critical thinking are welcome.*

We want to take an honest look at the issues and questions so common to this shared journey we all find ourselves on. We want to genuinely seek out what it means to follow Jesus in our ever-changing world, in our unfolding and expanding universe and in our pluralistic society.

We have come to know that doubt is not the enemy of faith, but rather that both doubt and curiosity are two of our biggest allies. We have learned that the Christian faith is more about wisdom and love than it is about correct doctrine or belief. And we believe that we are being invited to continually seek out both wisdom and love, renewing our minds, expanding our hearts and rethinking our faith in the process.

Thank you for joining us on that journey."

Why I Had to (Re)think Hell

When it comes to rethinking hell, the reasons are legion. (Haha, see what I did there.) Throughout this book, the other contributors show and demonstrate why rethinking hell is worth our time and what that could look like pragmatically. With that in mind, I would like to share with you a few of the reasons I had to rethink hell, unique to my experience.

For me, the belief in hell has played into what I like to refer to as the myth or illusion of separation. The truth is, we are all connected. I am deeply connected to my neighbor, I am deeply connected to creation, I am deeply connected to God and so are you. The mystics of various faith traditions have been telling us this for thousands of years, and the study of quantum physics has been confirming these ideas.

It is my conviction that it is the illusion of separateness that leads to sin. When I believe that I am separate from my neighbor, it allows me to dehumanize them, to be racist, to enslave them and even to kill them. The illusion that we are separate from creation has led to the denial of the climate crisis and the raping and pillaging of the earth. The illusion of separateness from God has cut us off from knowing who we truly are and has created a whole host of individuals who are deeply religious, but not spiritual.

I realized that how I think about and talk about hell has the potential to feed into this myth of separation. This deep interconnectedness is what Thich Nhat Hanh referred to as "interbeing,"[9] what the Nguni Bantu term "Ubuntu" ('I am because you are') is pointing to, and what Thomas Keating was getting at when he said, "The root of violence is the illusion of separation—from God, from Being itself, and from being one with everyone and everything."[10]

Another pressing issue with hell arises for me when I consider the God that I experience. When I engage in centering prayer and other contemplative practices, the God that I encounter is a God of Love. During my times of contemplation, it has become easy for me to slip into a state of deep oneness with creation and the entire universe. It is here that I feel a deep sense of love from God as I become aware of the deepest, truest aspect of who I am, Divine Love.

Because of these experiences, the belief in hell makes no sense to me. The deep sense of oneness with the universe and with God does not allow for something like hell. In order for me to buy into something like hell, unless we are talking about the very real hell we create here on earth, I would have to deny my experience of the Divine and that is simply not something I am willing to do.

I also find that the doctrine of hell is deeply anthropocentric and leads to an anemic theology that does not take the rest of creation and the universe into consideration. The universe is constantly growing and expanding. The earth is not the center of the universe and neither are people. There will be a time when humanity no longer walks the face of this earth... what then does the doctrine of hell even mean? Our theology within Western Christianity needs to break out of this anthropocentric perspective not only

9. Thich Nhất Hạnh, *Interbeing: The 14 Mindfulness Trainings of Engaged Buddhism* (Berkeley, CA: Parallax, 2020).

10. "Daily Meditation: The Root of Violence." Center for Action and Contemplation, May 1, 2022. https://cac.org/daily-meditations/the-root-of-violence-2022-05-01/.

when it comes to the doctrine of hell, but within the rest of our theology as well.

Finally, the most compelling reason I had to rethink my concept of hell is simply this: what does my concept of hell say about the God I worship? Our image and view of God is perhaps the most important aspect of who we are and what theology we hold. Our image of God impacts every other aspect of our theology. What does it do to our theology when we believe that the God we say is love, is willing to sustain the life and soul of those who failed the cosmic theology test on earth, simply so they could be tortured in hell consciously and for eternity?

What does it do to our theology when the God who decided not to be God without us via the incarnation, decides to destroy those very same individuals God apparently came to save? In what meaningful way can we say that God is Love, or just, or wants to be with us? What violence and atrocities are justified on our behalf when we believe that the God we worship tortures people in hell forever? What has been the fruit of the church's teachings on hell?

At the end of the day, I have no access to what happens when we die. I really don't know what I think about the afterlife, my beliefs there are not settled and probably never will be. But I do still have faith. I have faith towards a God who is love. I have faith towards a God who decided they did not want to be God without us. I have faith towards a God who is present in and through all things at all times seeking to bring about the most good and beauty and truth in all situations. That to me is a God worth being in relationship with. That to me is a God worth giving my life to.

CHAPTER 14

A Gospel of Hope: A Gentle Parenting Approach to Deconstructing Hell

Elizabeth Enns-Petters

I remember the smell of the chairs in the sanctuary as I bowed my head into them to plead for my eternal safety. I was six years old at most, and it wasn't even the first time I'd spoken the words of a prayer that I was taught alone can save me. I was afraid. The fiery flames of a place in the depth of the earth's core was a thing of nightmares-come-true. For the majority of my life, the purpose of Jesus and my relationship with my higher power was to keep me from Hell. Who wouldn't want to do everything possible to stay away from the fate of eternal conscious torment?

I shudder to think about this now and the many nights I spent obsessively praying to a God I pictured as an angrier version of Thor. Not immediately scary, but ready to take me down if I made a wrong move. I was confused. On the one hand, I wanted God to save me from harm, but on the other hand, I lived in fear of not being "chosen." I was told that heaven is my *hope*. So, what if I didn't make it there?

There are many belief systems and biblical interpretations when it comes to eternity. Universalism, infernalism, and annihilationism are just a few of the positions that Christians take when it comes to Hell. All three of them claim to be based in biblical truth. They are all rooted in a belief system that, in some way, can be interpreted to be backed by the Bible. The Bible seems to contradict itself at every other turn, so this is not a surprise. But the reality that there are so many differently held beliefs about Hell that I was not privy to in my formative years, gave me *hope* that I actually had the ability to CHOOSE the one that best fit my understanding of who God is.

As a child who suffered from debilitating anxiety (I wonder why…), the *hope* of Heaven was one that I was desperate to cling to. The world was a hard, scary place. I looked towards Heaven every day. But in order for Heaven to exist for those who had the right beliefs, who had said the right prayer, and who had done the right things, there had to be Hell for the others. There was just as much of a possibility that I could end up in that place of suffering and pain. Where then, was *hope*? Peace? Safety? Who was this God whose love was unconditional, but somehow also conditional?

The reality of differing theories about what happens after death was quite intriguing to me, a young person desperate to make sense of an all-loving God who also apparently sent people to eternal flames. I felt incredibly brave, sneaking around the evangelical Church to find eternal *hope*. But in hindsight, this possibility that God might actually be all-loving and all-merciful, saved my wavering faith and kept the spark of *hope* alive inside me.

What is Gentle Parenting?

As I became a parent, so much of what I began to learn about God's love was directly related to my launch into the practice of gentle parenting. The primary goal of this parenting style is to raise children with a focus on age-appropriate development. Gentile parenting largely embodies the idea that children deserve respect, empathy, and understanding as well as healthy boundaries. Gone are the days of children being "seen and not heard." Gentle parenting emphasizes that children should be treated as whole people with great emphasis on their developmental ability to process relationships and the world around them.

Learning to approach my kids with this mindset has convinced me that it's much more effective to draw my kids close than it is to push them away. They blossom under firm and loving direction, and so I try to give them that kind of direction.

If I, as a flawed human being, want to parent my children in a way that they will both understand and thrive under, then why would God not desire to create the same environment for us? What if God is the ultimate gentle parent? What if God leads with respect, empathy and understanding, along with structure and healthy boundaries? And if that is true, then where exactly does Hell fit in?

Some have said that letting go of the belief of Hell as a literal place of eternal torment will cause everyone to do whatever they want, and there will be no control. Of course, it's quite true that there would be no control, but what I've found is that a lack of control isn't what leads to chaos and destruction. A lack of nurturing love and support does. We don't need more control; we need respectful, empathetic direction. We don't need more punishment; we need more grace. We don't need more anger; we need more peace. When I am able to parent my children this way, they thrive. So why wouldn't this also be true of God's relationship with us? If I am not sending my kids to their room, pushing them away, but drawing them close by snuggling with a book (or a movie), or gently holding their hands so they cannot hit, and they are thriving in that environment, then I cannot believe in a God who would push me away below the earth's core to be eternally separated from his love.

Gentle parenting is largely based on these four core ideals: empathy, respect, understanding, and boundaries.[1] Prioritizing all

---

1. According to Cleveland Clinic: How to Set Healthy Boundaries in Relationships (2022), "the goal of gentle parenting is to raise confident, independent and happy children through empathy, respect and understanding, and setting healthy boundaries." https://health.clevelandclinic.org/how-to-set-boundaries/

four of these ideals when parenting is not only important, but life changing. It offers our children the opportunity to form their own thoughts and feelings, to feel safe within their own bodies, and to experience healthy relationships. In a nutshell, it helps to foster what we need from God: a divine sense of *hope* and assurance.

EMPATHY

One of the many well-known practices of gentle parenting is empathy. In her book *Atlas of the Heart,* Brené Brown says that empathy "is an emotional skill set that allows us to understand what someone is experiencing and to reflect back that understanding."[2] She states elsewhere, "rather than walking in your shoes, I learn to listen to the story you tell about what it's like in your shoes and believe you even when it doesn't match my experiences."[3] Empathy is a great gift. It allows for a deep connection between two human beings who might not have experienced the same circumstances.

Empathy is human, and yet somehow divine. Who do we believe to be human and yet divine? Ah yes, Jesus of Nazareth. "For we do not have a High Priest who cannot empathize with our weaknesses, but we have one who has been tempted in every way-as we are-yet he did not sin."[4] A God who can empathize with their creation? That had never happened before. We are shown over and over throughout the life of Jesus (both biblical and historical accounts), that he was the epitome of empathy, a form of unconditional love.

John 11 accounts the story of Lazarus and his death. After getting word that Lazarus is dying, Jesus goes back to Judea. Along the

---

2. According to Brown, "empathy is not relating to an experience, it's connecting to what someone is feeling about an experience." *Atlas of the Heart* (New York: Random House, 2021), 120.

3. Brown states that "rather that walking in your shoes, I need to learn how to listen to the story you tell about what it's like in your shoes and believe you even when it doesn't match my experiences" (123)

4. Heb. 4:15 (NIV).

way he talks to his disciples of Lazarus' death. He had been in the tomb four days already upon Jesus' arrival. The sisters, Mary and Martha accompany Jesus to the tomb. Verse 33 says that Jesus was "deeply moved in spirit and troubled" when he saw Mary and the others crying. Verse 38 tells us that upon arrival at the tomb, Jesus was "once more deeply moved" and in verse 35, "Jesus wept."

He was going to raise Lazarus from the dead. He had told his disciples that from the beginning, so he really has nothing to be sad about. But the sadness and intensity of the grief that surrounded him moved him to tears. Jesus the healer, but also Jesus the empath.

If Jesus is God incarnate, and he showed empathy during his time on earth, it's safe to assume that God empathizes with us as well. How then would this same God let any of us suffer eternal damnation? It just doesn't add up. God is the master of empathy, able to see so far into our souls that they can empathize with all of it. For me, that is enough. That kind of empathy is the key to the unconditional love we have in Christ, no need for a special prayer from a little girl in a church sanctuary. Empathy stirs *hope*.

RESPECT

I recently reclaimed the word "respect." For a long time, I was confused about what respect actually meant. When it rolled off of my tongue, it felt like a middle-aged white man demanding that I worship him. The more I wander down this path of parenting my children and re-parenting myself, the more that I find that respect is vital. Respect is a key part of gentle parenting and it's a key part of the human experience. A large portion of the atrocities we have seen our world face is because of the disrespect between groups of people. It should not be overlooked.

I am always quite drawn to Jesus' interaction with the Samaritan woman.[5] The Bible refers often to hatred between

---

5. John 4 (NIV).

Jews and Samaritans.[6] When Israel fell to the Assyrians in 722 B.C.E.[7], those left in Israel married foreigners and their offspring, these half-Jewish, half-Gentile people are what became known as Samaritans. They created a religion that the Jews believed to be heresy. Samaritans were a mixed-race people who defied the "one true religion" of the Jews.

When Jesus meets a Samaritan at a well, and a woman no less, it would have made sense that he would either avoid her or mock her. And yet, he asks her for water. As readers of the story, we discover that this woman is also of questionable morality according to the culture, and Jesus knows this as well. Still, he asks for a drink and engages the woman in conversation as he would anyone else. She is so eager to listen, to learn, to hear more of what he has to say. In many ways, it seems absurd that she would hear his words and trust him enough to go tell the entire village of what he spoke. Perhaps it was because he first respected her in this bold and beautiful way. He gave worth to her feeling of worthlessness, and she was willing to listen further. He gave her much-needed *hope*.

Respect is a gateway to healthy relationships. When we are respected, we feel safe, heard, known. When I am not respected by someone, I shut down or I run. I definitely don't stand by and hear what they have to say. We can't disrespect others and expect them to trust us; Jesus knew this, and God knows this.

UNDERSTANDING

We all like to be understood. A moment of misunderstanding feels like agony, especially to my fellow social anxiety sufferers. I would gladly give my left arm (I am right-handed, but still!) to never be misunderstood again. When I speak of the relationships that I

---

6. Neh. 6:1-14 is when the Bible first references the relationship between Samaritans and Jews.

7. Ido Koch, "Assyrian Deportation and Resettlement: The Story of Samaria," *The Torah. com*, 2019, https://www.thetorah.com/article/assyrian-deportation-and-resettlement-the-story-of-samaria.

value the most, the people I feel closest to, I most always describe how understood I feel by that person.

Understanding is being "sympathetically aware of other people's feelings."[8] Whether it comes to my emotional, spiritual, social, and academic knowledge, I want others to understand what I am saying and how I feel about it. This act of understanding requires listening and asking questions. It requires investment in both the topic and the person. Understanding doesn't require agreement; it just requires presence. It is such an incredible act of love, sitting with someone whose views differ from ours and understanding where they are coming from. Conversations like these often leave me feeling closer to the divine and give me the *hope* that I need.

Jesus spent much of his time with outcasts and "sinners." A common belief is that he did this because he was finding the lost sheep and building his church. This does not feel right to me. It does not do justice to the character of Jesus, and leaves us to believe that our only job is to bring the lost to church and then we are done. This seems out of character with the nature of Jesus, the man who made a point of having relationships with societal and religious outcasts: eating dinner with a tax collector, conversing with a Samaritan adulteress at a well, sharing supper with his betrayer. Jesus spent a significant amount of time with these people, and from what I can see, he seemed to ask them lots of questions and listened intently for their response. He sought to understand them, their world and what had gotten them to the place they were in.

He shows that God listens without interrupting, allows us to process how we need to process, and who sits with us in curiosity. This is not a God who would condemn people to the fiery pits of hell because of differing views, lifestyles, and understandings of the world. That doesn't quite add up.

---

8. *Oxford English Dictionary,* 2nd ed. (Oxford: Oxford University Press, 2004), s.v. "Understanding."

BOUNDARIES

Boundaries are physical, mental, emotional, and spiritual. Boundaries protect us and others. Without boundaries, we lose our sense of self. Where we stop and where others begin becomes very confusing and harmful. Fostering good, healthy boundaries is one of the most important things I am trying to teach my children. I want them to be able to assess their needs and then create boundaries around those needs in order to keep them sacred.

My very favorite of Jesus' characteristics is his ability to make and keep boundaries. They're so clear, so gentle, and kept without apology.

I often wondered as a child why Jesus didn't just heal everybody. What was he doing just hanging around the same places and healing only a handful of those who were hurting? What was up with him? I had a deep love for Superman during that time and wanted God to be my superhero, to come through for me and those around me. But what I found was that Jesus didn't operate like that. He spent lots of time alone, connecting with God in prayer.[9] In John 4, we read that he grew weary, and that he rested. Jesus turned crowds away to guard his sacred and needed time of prayer. I can imagine it was not always met with understanding and grace, especially from people that came from miles and miles just to see him, hoping he would be their superhero. But Jesus knew that part of being human was being limited, and that required making good space for alone time.

Jesus urged us in Matthew 11:28-30 "Come to me, all who are weary and burdened, and I will give you rest. Take my yoke upon you and learn from me, for I am gentle and humble in heart, and you will find rest for your souls. For my yoke is easy and my burden is light."

Count me in for that kind of peace and safety. Jesus invited us to experience rest, to lay down our burdens and come to him

---

9. Luke 9:18 (NIV).

vulnerable and weary. That requires a level of safety and trust and need. That offering is not a trap; there's no hidden meaning or agenda. That offering guides us into a gentle *hope*. Just come and rest and know that though this life is hard, he won't pull the rug out from under us. We don't have to keep the divine at a distance for fear that we cannot trust them with our eternity.

A Gospel of Hope

My lack of ability to trust God in my formative years is one of the biggest things I keep coming back to as I deconstruct my belief in a literal Hell. I created walls and moats all around me because God just seemed completely mad, and not to be trusted. Everything that I did felt like one more nail in my coffin. If God was all-knowing and I was screwing up all over the place, then eternity did not look great for me. It never even crossed my mind that God might allow me to be myself, and that somehow God was secure enough in who they were to give me appropriate space and not be tallying up my shortcomings.

What if who we are isn't completely tied up in who God is? What if there's a beautiful boundary there? What if God doesn't take everything we do personally but approaches us with empathy, respect, and understanding? What if we can trust God to keep us safe and to honor our needs? What if it's not all about God? What if it's a little bit about us too, and that's how God always meant it to be?

I have learned that the things my soul deeply longs for are okay. The empathy, and respect, and understanding, and healthy boundaries that I need, are valid. People have asked me, "How do you know what God is like?" My answer is very simple, "I don't. But I will continue to believe that whoever makes me feel safe and loved and beautifully whole, is who God is."

If the God of my childhood was ready to use his belt on me every chance they got, then the God of my now is there with open arms as I cry out in fear. They are not a Greek god, exercising their powers on human beings as they wish, for their own vengeance or pleasure, but a God who broke all the historical "rules" on who a god should be. They are not a god who throws people into fire pits for all eternity, but a God who ushers his people into a place of healing and wholeness and freedom. If I wanted a Greek god, I'd worship Zeus (he's pretty cool, right?). But what I desire and what I thrive under, just as my kids do, is a loving and nurturing relationship with a higher power.

Hope depends on this truth. "Hope presumes nothing but is rooted in deeper confidence: the love and mercy of an openhearted and relentlessly kind God."[10]

If God as our creator fashioned us to be like him, then wouldn't the most beautiful of human attributes be found in God as well? All the love, safety, and security of the healthiest relationship we could ever imagine: that is God. That is the *hope* of Christ, the *hope* of eternity, the *hope* that needs no Hell to back it up. "For I am convinced that neither death nor life, neither angels nor demons, neither the present nor the future, nor any powers, neither height not depth, nor anything else in all creation, will be able to separate us from the love of God that is in Christ Jesus our Lord."[11]

If nothing can separate us from the love of Christ, then Hell makes no sense. It's the most beautiful story ever told. One where we are all held, safe, and unconditionally loved. That is the *hope* of the Gospel.

---

10. Bradley Jersak, *Her Gates Will Never be Shut: Hope, Hell, and the New Jerusalem* (Eugene, OR: Wipf & Stock, 2010), 10.

11. Rom. 8:38-39 (NIV).

CHAPTER 15

Pushed by Fear or Led by Love?

Esther Joy Goetz

A nine-year old girl lays awake on the top bunk in a dorm room in a far-away, war-torn country, asking Jesus into her heart for what she really hopes is the final time, but it will probably happen again the next night. She clutches her Raggedy-Ann doll tightly to her chest, tears streaming down her face under cover of darkness. Mommy and Daddy are far away preaching the "gospel" to those who haven't heard. Even though she wishes she could call out for them in that moment, she tells herself over and over again that this is a good thing and this is what God wants because, like all the grownups keep saying around her, "we are all playing a part in saving the lost from Hell," the lake of fire that burns forever and ever. "But what if I'm lost?" she asks herself as she drifts off to another nightmare-filled and fitful sleep.

Many years later and continents away, another nine-year old girl races into her aunt's bedroom in the middle of the night, awakened by a terrifying nightmare. Her own mommy has just died several days before after a long battle with cancer, and this getaway is supposed to give her daddy some space to get the house in order. All she has heard these last several months is how, "mommy is going to be with Jesus because she has been elected from before the foundation of the world and this is God's will." Her daddy preached at the funeral about how not to go to Hell, that place of eternal pain and separation from God, and how to be in heaven with mommy. All anyone has to do is repent and believe the gospel. She's confused because she had heard in church that God chooses some and not others, and since it's all up to Him, whatever brings Him the most glory is what will happen. "What if I'm not one of the elect," she sobs into her aunt's chest, "what if God hasn't chosen me and I never see my mommy again?"

I am the missionary kid and I am the aunt.

———◆◆———

These stories, while heart-breaking, are commonplace, especially in the arena of evangelicalism, Hell and children.

They represent so many stories of children being told about the scariest of all spaces, "the place of nightmares," as my one friend's daughter was told in her first-grade Christian school classroom, and the impending fiery and separation-from-God doom that will accompany them upon death if they don't _____ (fill in the blank with whatever particular sect of religion is part of that child's life).

It might be why your heart began to race and your palms became sweaty as you read those first two paragraphs of this chapter. In many ways, this is your story too, and your amygdala, the part of your brain that feels fear at a primal level, wants to protect that little child part of you again.

Every religion, at its core, begins with an ideology of what we should be fearful of.

Their solutions give an answer of promised peace and no more fear. Usually the means is control, especially of beliefs and behavior. Religion controls the narrative, the behavior and the outcome.

Just do this or that and we will be saved from whatever terrible thing awaits us. For the evangelical Christian, this FEAR and subsequent control is at the root of the doctrine of Hell. Well-meaning parents, including me, tend to be pushed into it and by it.

Fear of death.

Verses like "For the wages of sin is death,"[1] (it was one of the very first verses I memorized in my formative years) validates the idea that the world and the God who made it are very unsafe.

Fear of abandonment by God.

Children are told they are separated from God (think cute comic strips like the "Four Spiritual Laws"[2]) and there is the definite possibility that they will be separated forever. No wonder children do not feel like they belong, and struggle to find a way to belong their whole lives.

Fear of separation from those we love.

When my niece came to me that night terrified that she would be separated from her mommy forever, my heart shattered. One of the core needs a child has is that they will not be abandoned by those who care for them, who love them and who they belong to. To place that eternal threat over a child in order to coerce them into believing a set of tenets or doctrines is a great form of child manipulation and abuse.

Fear of punishment.

The system of rewards and punishment used in the behavior management of children is very mainstream. Children don't have the tools yet for intrinsic motivation and oftentimes, punishment seems to be the only option on the table. Research is slowly finding that punishment which, again, taps into the primal brain stem

---

1. Rom. 6:23 (NIV).
2. Bill Bright, "The Four Spiritual Laws," *Campus Ministry Today* (August 1994).

where fear resides, only provides a temporary and unhealthy solution and actually hinders the ability to learn and grow and thrive. Fear of punishment works to manage external behavior immediately, and that's why parents are so tempted to use it.

Fear of endless pain and suffering.

Wailing and gnashing of teeth and a lake of fire that burns forever and ever is the most damaging of all the teachings surrounding Hell when it comes to children. For children to be thrust into even the notion of extreme violence and eternal torture and for it to be tethered to a God who supposedly loves them creates confusion and distrust and fosters anxiety, shame, and depression. How could it not?

As I began raising my four children, I fell into this trap. I was afraid, pushed by fear.

Having been raised under a very conservative evangelical system, I believed wholeheartedly in the literal eternal conscious torment of those who did not "place their faith" in the atoning work of Jesus on the cross. I had been born bad, did bad things and those bad things (and me along with them) were responsible for the death of the precious and beloved Son of God. If I didn't believe in this particular version of Jesus or trust my soul to this narrowly defined form of him, then I was headed to Hell when I died.

When I began my parenting, I took this ideology with me. My children were sinful at their core (their "hearts were deceitful above all things and desperately wicked"[3]) and were part of the collective responsibility for the death of Jesus. They were headed to Hell unless I did my part in evangelizing them. Thus, my main mission in parenting was born: keep my children from going to Hell.

It didn't matter how scared I made them; I was telling them the truth. It didn't matter how much anxiety they had about it all; I was doing my job as a good Christian mom. It didn't matter how

---

3. Jer. 17:9 (NIV).

damaging this was to their person; this life was short and I was saving them for the only thing that mattered: the afterlife. I was afraid and they should be too. Hell was, as Richard Rohr notes, something "ultimate and urgent"[4] and I would be remiss if I didn't warn them about it.

I repeated these caveats over and over to myself as I watched the damage unfold with my oldest. She was petrified of leaving me even through high school. She developed the compulsive habit of confession (to me) of every possible sin imaginable, many which were just normal childhood thoughts and behaviors. She held her four-year-old brother down in the back of the car until he said the "magic prayer" because she was beside herself that he was going to die without having asked Jesus into his heart and she would be responsible for him suffering forever.

I feel sickened thinking of that now, but that is what was true.

Fear ruled my life and subsequently, the lives of my children. And the fear of Hell was always at the forefront.

I've often wondered why we, as the human race, are so addicted to fear. I've come to the possible notion that fear allows us to stay in the easy place of simplistic thinking and subsequent action: we deem what is dangerous and come up with a solution for what we can do about it. If we figure out what is unsafe, we can figure out how to make ourselves safe again. It makes sense then why, when fear rules, the desire to quiet it with the tool of control moves to the forefront, as it did voraciously in my own parenting.

I controlled my kids' every behavior, threatening them with temporal punishment as my God-given right. If God punishes us to get us to do what He wants, then I have utter permission and downright urging as His representative and authority over my children to do the same.

I controlled what they listened to, read, watched and memorized, which happened to be only Christian songs, books, videos

---

4. Richard Rohr, host, "Hell, the Devil and the Afterlife," Another Name for Everything (podcast), August 17, 2019, https://cac.org/podcasts/3-hell-the-devil-and-the-afterlife/.

and Bible verses. The fear of them being exposed to anything else ate me alive inside. After all, it may start them on the "wide road that leads to destruction" and I was responsible for taking them down the "narrow path that leads to life."[5]

I controlled who they were allowed to be with, what we did on Sundays and Wednesdays and Friday nights, all with the vain attempt to squelch any possibility of them becoming out of control.

To be honest, I don't blame myself for this fear that was put into me at such a young age and all the control that came as a natural byproduct of that. If eternal conscious torment in Hell was true, of course I would NOT want that for my kids and as a good parent, I would do everything in my power to make sure none of that happened. It felt like fear and its companion of control were my best options. What else was there?

I remember the day standing on the sidelines with a friend at a track meet. We were watching our girls pound the pavement when she challenged my idea of Hell as eternal conscious torment. This was someone who knew their Bible inside and out, and who I trusted as a wise source for spiritual direction.

On the way home in the car, I asked my then 13-year-old about it. "What do you think about Hell, honey?" Having only my evangelical verbiage to use, I then asked her, "Which would bring God more glory: some people in Hell or no people there?"

Her answer began a slow change in my heart. "Mom, I believe that it makes God's love shine more brightly and reveals how big His love is if there is no one beyond the reach of it. No matter what we've said or done. And once we are confronted with such a great and unconditional love, we would never want to resist it. I believe people are in Hell here in this life because they don't know how to receive that love and maybe when all that's blocking them is gone, that will be heaven."

This particular child, who I called "unconditional love in a body" played a big part in that moment of leading me away from

---

5. Matthew 7:13 (NIV).

the stranglehold of fear and toward the much better path of being led by love.

My questions arose at every turn.

What if there is no eternal conscious torment? What if it's been a marketing scheme to keep me and my kids in line?

What if, for many, Hell is here and now? What if the whole point is to interrupt this Hell and bring the kingdom of heaven to earth,[6] as Jesus prayed?

What if I don't have to be afraid for myself? For my kids?

What if I can love my own children without this agenda to get them saved?

What if God wants me to stop being pushed by fear and instead led by love in all my parenting decisions?

What if all those times Jesus said "do not fear,"[7] He understood our tendency to be ruled by it and act from it and how bad that was for us and those we love?

It was as if the floodgates opened wide and I was free to wonder, to ask, to change my mind and to figure out a whole new way to parent: one rooted and grounded in love. Used to being the "answer" girl, those questions provided just the right medium for me to dream of another possibility.

I don't remember the exact moment, but I do remember the feeling of exuberance and freedom that came when I took Hell off the table, or more correctly, eternal conscious torment. It was as if the unbearable weight I had been carrying unwittingly and as the underpinning for all of my parenting was lifted and tossed into the deepest part of the ocean.

---

6. Matthew 6:10(NIV).

7. Luke 12:32 (NIV).

I was actually free.

Free to think new thoughts, motivated not by the normal and harmful reaction of fear and control, but by a much healthier response to love.

During those early weeks and months, I had to practice this new way of thinking, almost forming new neural pathways in my brain. I started with strangers, (e.g., the Muslim man at the gas station who treated me with extraordinary kindness). I would say to whoever was in the car very sarcastically, "He's going to Hell, right?!? I better hand him this gospel pamphlet I happen to have in the glove compartment." And then we would laugh and laugh mostly at our former selves forever believing that way.

It was easy to begin to change my thought patterns when it came to those I didn't know because I had no stake in the emotional game about their eternal destiny.

But then I moved to my neighbors, especially the ones who did not "know Jesus." Could I love them with no strings attached, without that agenda of getting them saved? I practiced some more, working through the strongholds of evangelism that had been burned into my very young brain. I watched their kids and mustered up my courage not to invite them to the church family movie night, reminding myself again that no matter what, no one was headed to eternal conscious torment. I talked with deconstructing friends about the niggling fear in the back of my brain that I was not doing my proper Christian duty and they would offer to cheer me on every time I just loved with no ulterior motive, reminding me that God loves that way and it's the most beautiful.

When it finally came down to it, the hardest space for me was with my kids. This vow I had made to keep them out of Hell had controlled me for so long. Fear of making the wrong decision, being a terrible parent and my children suffering for eternity because of my lack of belief in Hell paralyzed me for a time. I felt stuck between this space of knowing that any parenting that uses fear as a motivator and control as a manipulator is not good, right or healthy AND the haunting place of "what if I'm wrong?"

But as I slowly unpacked and untangled this fear/love knot that seemed to be balled up within me, the choice became ever obvious: make in-the-moment choices every day in every area of my life, including and especially in my parenting, to be led by love and not pushed by fear.

This would not be an easy venture, as changing is one of the most difficult parts of being human, but one that is well worth all the risk associated with being taken by the hand by Love Themself. It meant upending all the systems that had served me for so long:

- Doing away with eternal conscious torment and the fear motivator behind it in all my conversations with my children.

- Moving to the much more nuanced and complicated way of responding with love and not reacting with fear in both the small and big decisions of daily parental life.

- Loving my children with no agenda, seeking to give them the roots of unconditional love and the wings of freedom to be completely themselves, however that played out moment-by-moment and year-by-year.

- Putting myself in the position of both learner and teacher in my relationship with my children, so that we could ask questions together and allow for different conclusions.

- Letting go of control over my children's eternal destiny and trusting the process of choosing love in the here and now.

- Being present and mindful of what was happening, both good and bad, to my children here on earth, not focused and distracted by what might come in some later ethereal time period in a far-off place.

The good news is that, in our family, we all found out that love, in the end, is a much more powerful force than fear. When we choose to love, we experience goodness, life, healing, restoration, kindness, joy, patience, peace, connection and freedom.

As I began to unravel the fear-driven beliefs about God and I clung to the ones that spoke of their unconditional love, I felt held, safe and free to be me.

And if I was held, safe and free to be me without that dreaded mean monster of fear controlling my every thought, word and move, I could pass these very good gifts along to my kids.

Death is scary but it's not the end.

I come from love, am held in love and will return to love. Death, as CS Lewis writes, is the invitation to "come further up and further in"[8] to love. Love is the energy and force that binds me to God and others, protects me, and keeps me safe (on the inside, where my soul dwells and forever, where it ultimately matters). It's the same for my kids.

I am not and never will be abandoned by God.

I am "rooted and established in the wide, long, high and deep love of Christ, that surpasses knowledge."[9] I have freedom to live FROM that place of belonging instead of FOR it. So do my kids.

I am not and will not be separated from those I love.

We are all one in Christ and we are all connected at a deep and fundamental level, and there is nothing powerful enough to change that. That oneness holds us all through time and eternity because it is driven by God Themself. My kids are part of that "one us."

---

8. C.S. Lewis. *The Lion, the Witch and the Wardrobe.* (London: Geoffrey Bles, 1950).
9. Ephesians 3:18-19 (NIV).

Love does not punish.

Punishment is only used as a behavior management tool and is not grounded in and from a place of love, only control. God has no need for it as They cannot control and love us at the same time. My kids are loved, not controlled by God.

I will not be in eternal conscious torment forever.

I am and will be enveloped in love. The love that is gentle and kind. The love that is peaceful and restorative. The love that is patient and faithful. The love that fosters hope and trust. The love that Jesus exemplified. The love that never fails. So are and will be my kids.

As I soaked these beautiful truths into my soul, and believed that my kids were held, safe and free to be perfectly themselves without Hell staring us down like a lion on the prowl, ready to devour us at any moment, my fear slowly dissipated, my desire to control took a backseat and love moved to the forefront.

This has not been quick or easy. It still is not. It's much quicker and easier to live in fear and grasp tightly to the illusion of control. It's been a long, hard-fought road to think differently, to heal and to embrace a new reality as a parent with Hell off the table. When I falter (which feels almost daily), the question I come back to again and again is this one: "Am I being pushed by fear or led by love?"[10] I am wise to listen to the answer.

A nine-year old girl lays awake on the top bunk in a dorm room in a far-away, war-torn country, whimpering into her pillow. Her dorm mother hears her cries and comes to sit at her bedside. "What's wrong, my sweet girl?" she asks gently. "I'm afraid," she sheepishly

---

10. Emily P. Freeman, "Do This Before Every Hard Decision," The Next Right Thing (podcast), August 15, 2017, https://emilypfreeman.com/podcast/ep-02/.

shares through her sobs as she falls into the waiting arms of this woman she has come to trust. "What if the people with guns come to get us tonight and I die? What will happen?" The young lady, entrusted with the care of this little one, strokes her hair and lovingly walks her through the exercise they learned earlier in the day, "Take a long deep breath in and then slowly breathe out. We can do it together if you'd like for as long as you need. I'm not going anywhere. And remember, when we breathe in, we are breathing in the very big love of God and we are breathing out the very big love of God. They are with us with every single breath we take, in and out, in and out." After a few minutes, the little girl's heart rate slows, her body relaxes, and she drifts off to sleep knowing she is safe and loved.

Many years later and continents away, another nine-year old girl races into her aunt's bedroom in the middle of the night, awakened by a terrifying nightmare. Her very own mommy has just died several days before after a long battle with cancer, and this getaway is supposed to give her daddy the space to grieve without all the pressing needs of the family that he has tried so hard to hold together these past several months. "I'm so afraid, Aunt Esther. Will I see Mommy again?" Her aunt gathers her up into her arms and tells her, once again, that God loves her and is very sad for what is happening to her, that They are with her with every breath she takes, beside her with all the tears she cries and They are never leaving her, even during nightmares. She reminds her about what Daddy said at the funeral about how much he loves and misses Mommy, but that one day, they will all be together again with Jesus and it will be so happy, but that it's really okay to be very sad now. She turns the nightlight on and scratches her niece's back until she finally closes her eyes in sleep. The aunt lays down on the floor next to the bed, shedding her own very heart-broken tears.

About the Authors

Chad Bahl is a Christian schooled in the Evangelical tradition and currently pursuing his doctorate in Theology/Ministry at Northwind Theological Seminary. He is author of *God Unbound: An Evangelical Reconsiders Tradition in Search of Truth*. Bahl authors the blog TheLayTheologian.com and teaches systematic theology at a large multi-campus church.

Sharon L. Baker Putt is Professor of Theology and Religion at Messiah University. She holds a Ph.D. from Southern Methodist University and is the author of *Razing Hell, Executing God*, and *A Nonviolent Theology of Love*.

Robert D. Cornwall is Minister-at-Large with standing in the Christian Church (Disciples of Christ), having retired as pastor of Central Woodward Christian Church of Troy, Michigan in June 2021. He holds a Ph.D. in Historical Theology from Fuller Theological Seminary, is a blogger, editor, & the author of a growing number of books.

Elizabeth Enns Petters (Lizz), is a freelance writer and a podcaster known for the Deconstructing Mamas Podcast. Most days she can be found cleaning goldfish off the bottom of her feet as she tries to keep up with her two young children.

Julie Ferwerda is an author and holistic nurse dedicated to helping others overcome fear and disease through rediscovery of their invincible connections to God, Self, and others. She is the author of several books including, *Raising Hell: Christianity's Most Controversial Doctrine Put Under Fire*. She currently lives in the mountains of Puerto Rico where she conducts spiritual and leisure retreats.

Keith Giles is a former pastor who abandoned the pulpit to follow Jesus and ended up founding a church where 100% of the offering was given away to help the poor in the community. He is the author of the 7-part best-selling Jesus Un book series, including *Jesus Undefeated: Condemning the False Doctrine of Eternal Torment*, and of the book *Sola Mysterium: Celebrating the Beautiful Uncertainty of Everything*. He lives with his wife, Wendy in El Paso, Texas.

Esther Goetz is a co-host for the Deconstructing Mamas podcast, a freelance writer, speaker and faith coach. Having been raised as a missionary kid in war-torn Ethiopia, and then raising her own children in suburban New Jersey, she has a fierce passion to restore hope and healing to the sacred space where our hearts and our homes meet, including faith, marriage and motherhood. She unpacks her ever-evolving faith journey on social media as Esther, the Dolly Mama.

Meghan Henning is the Associate Professor of Christian Origins at the University of Dayton. She holds a Master's degree in Biblical Studies from Yale Divinity School, and a Doctorate in New Testament from Emory University. Meghan's first book on the pedagogical function of Hell in antiquity is entitled *Educating Early Christians through the Rhetoric of Hell* (Mohr Siebeck). Her second book, *Hell Hath No Fury: Gender, Disability and the Invention of Damned Bodies in Early Christianity* (Yale University Press), examines hell through the lenses of gender and disability studies. She is the recipient of grants and awards from the Jacob K. Javits foundation, the Society of Biblical Literature, Yale Divinity School, and Emory University and has appeared in a documentary for the National Geographic Channel and on CNN.

Dr. Mark Gregory Karris is a licensed marriage and family therapist in full-time private practice in San Diego, California. He is a husband, father, and recording artist. He's a voracious reader, researcher, and all-around biophilic. Mark is the author of the best-selling book *Religious Refugees: (De)Constructing Toward Spiritual and Emotional Healing* (Quoir, 2020). MarkGregoryKarris.com

Chris Loewen is pursuing an MDiv from Providence Theological Seminary while working full time in the Agriculture Industry as a Nutrient Management Planner. He lives with his wife, Diane, and their three young children in Blumenort, Manitoba, where he serves on the Preaching Team at Crossview Church.

R.T. Mullins (PhD, University of St Andrews) is a visiting professor of philosophy at Palm Beach Atlantic University and the University of Lucerne. He is the author of multiple books, and over 50 essays.

Thomas Jay Oord, Ph.D., is a theologian, philosopher, and scholar of multi-disciplinary studies. Oord directs the Center for Open and Relational Theology and a doctoral program at Northwind Theological Seminary. The author or editor of 25+ books, Oord lectures at institutions across the globe.

Joshua Patterson is the host of the (Re)thinking Faith podcast. He is an Open and Relational / Process thinker who has been deeply formed by the Mystical tradition within the Christian Faith. Faith seeking understanding continuously leads Josh on his journey of becoming.

Shawn M. Ryan, M.A. Theological Studies, is a non-vocational lay theologian and founder of Other Sheep Theology Group. Shawn is a one of the "Voices" for the Center for Open and Relational Theology and works to share with those in non-academic fields to connect with people in their personal and everyday environments.

Eric A. Seibert, Ph.D., is an author, speaker, and professor of Old Testament. Among his numerous publications are *Disturbing Divine Behavior* (2009), *The Violence of Scripture* (2012), *Disarming the Church* (2018), and *Enjoying the Old Testament* (2021). Seibert enjoys helping people wrestle with problematic portrayals of God in the Old Testament and encourages them to read the Bible in ways that promote peace.

ALSO FROM

SacraSage Press...

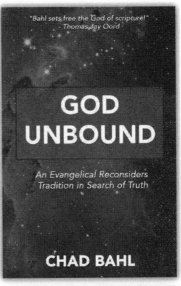

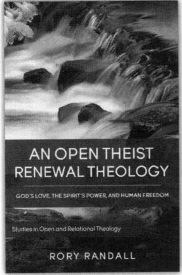

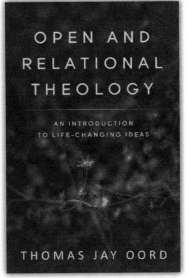

SACRASAGEPRESS.COM

ALSO FROM

SacraSage Press...

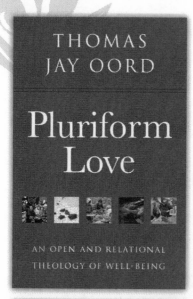

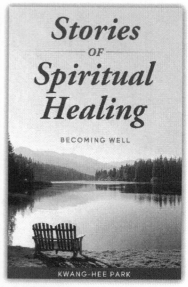

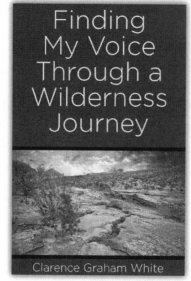

SACRASAGEPRESS.COM

Made in the USA
Columbia, SC
26 September 2023

23424729R00140